WHAT WILL HAPPEN IF...

WHAT WILL HAPPEN IF...

Young Children and the Scientific Method

By Barbara Sprung
Merle Froschl
Patricia B. Campbell

Developed by
Beginning Math and Science Equitably Project
Educational Equity Concepts, Inc.
New York 1985

Women's Educational Equity Act Program
U.S. Department of Education
William J. Bennett, Secretary

Cover and book design by Jim Anderson.

Photographs by Ann Chwatsky were taken at School Number Four, Lawrence Public Schools, Inwood, N.Y.

Additional photographs that appear on pages 42, 43, and 51 were taken by Ann-Marie Mott at the Bank Street Children's School, New York, N.Y. The photo on page 109 was taken by Neil M. Shively at the White Plains, (NY) Child Day Care Association, Inc.

Typeset by Jiffy Jenie Printing Center, Inc., Centereach, N.Y.

Printed by Arcata Graphics/Fairfield, Fairfield, PA.

Fifth printing, April 1991

Published by Educational Equity Concepts, Inc., New York, NY

Printed in U.S.A.

Distributed by Gryphon House, Inc., 3706 Otis Street, P.O. Box 275, Mt. Rainier, MD 20712.

Library of Congress Cataloging in Publication Data

Sprung, Barbara.
　　What will happen if—.

　　Bibliography: p.
　　1. Science—Study and teaching (Preschool)—United States. 2. Mathematics—Study and teaching—(Preschool) —United States. 3. Science—Study and teaching (Primary)—United States. 4. Mathematics—Study and teaching (Primary)—United States. 5. Educational equalization—United States. I. Froschl, Merle. II. Campbell, Patricia B. III. Title.
LB1140.5.S35S67　1985　　　372.3'5044　　　85-6872
ISBN 0-931-62902-0 (pbk.)

Discrimination Prohibited: No person in the United States shall, on the grounds of race, color or national origin, be excluded from participation in, be denied the benefits of, or be subjected to discrimination under any program or activity receiving Federal financial assistance, or be so treated on the basis of sex under most education programs or activities receiving Federal assistance.

The activity which is the subject of this report was produced under a grant from the U.S. Department of Education, under the auspices of the Women's Educational Equity Act. Opinions expressed herein do not necessarily reflect the position or policy of the Department, and no official endorsement should be inferred.

ACKNOWLEDGMENTS

Many individuals participated in the development of Beginning Math and Science Equitably and in the creation of this curriculum guide. We wish to take this opportunity to thank each and every person for her or his participation.

Special thanks to the children at School Number Four of the Lawrence New York Public Schools. Their enthusiastic response to the activities proved beyond a doubt that math, science, and technology enhance the preschool curriculum. Special thanks also to the administrators and teachers at School Number Four. Without their cooperation the pilot testing could not have taken place. They are: Sheila Terens, Principal; Pat Gray, Prekindergarten Director; and Sherri Shapiro, Frank Small, and Sylvia Webb, teachers who pilot tested the activities in their classrooms. We also want to thank Jill K. Wildenberg, science specialist, for allowing us to test the "Bottles and Liquids" activities in the school's Science Museum. We extend thanks to Louis Anne Yee, a staff member at the beginning of the Project, for her contribution to the development and pilot testing of the "Bottles and Liquids" activities. Finally, we thank all the teachers at School Number Four for participating in the inservice course that preceded the pilot testing and for their cooperation and helpful suggestions throughout.

Four Senior Consultants made an enormous contribution to the development of Beginning Math and Science Equitably. They are: Patricia B. Campbell of Campbell-Kibler Associates; Harriet K. Cuffaro, Graduate Faculty, Bank Street College of Education; Selma Greenberg, Professor of Education, Hofstra University; and Barbara Henriques, third-grade teacher at the St. Thomas School in New Haven, Connecticut. Their expertise informed and guided the project from planning for the Curriculum Development meeting at the beginning to critiquing this guide at the end. In addition to her role as senior consultant, Patricia Campbell served as Evaluator to the project and is a co-author of this guide. We wish to express our gratitude for her triple role, her tireless enthusiasm, and her unflagging good humor.

In addition to the Senior Consultants, we wish to thank Barbara Bowman, Director, Erikson Institute for Early Childhood, Chicago,

Illinois; Elizabeth Fennema, Department of Mathematics, University of Wisconsin at Madison; Nancy Kreinberg, Director, Project Equals, Lawrence Hall of Science, University of California at Berkeley; and Lisa A. Serbin, Department of Psychology, Concordia University, Montreal, Quebec. As members of the Advisory Committee they contributed to the Curriculum Development meeting that launched the Project and lent additional support throughout.

Many other individuals with a broad range of expertise attended the Curriculum Development meeting at the Project's inception, and we wish to thank them all for their significant contributions. They are: Leona Arnold, Helping Teacher, Early Childhood Center of the Freeport New York Public Schools; Mary Bondarin, Director, Early Childhood Center of the Freeport New York Public Schools; Linda Colón, Administrator, Educational Equity Concepts; Yvonne DeGaetano, Director, Cross Cultural Demonstration Project, Teachers College, Columbia University; John Hinton, Principal, Riverside Elementary School, Rockville Centre, New York; Lavinia Mancuso, Principal, P.S. 155, New York, New York; Ellen Rubin, Special Education Staff Specialist, Educational Equity Concepts; George Tokieda, Science Specialist, Brearley School, New York, New York; and Bernard Zubrowski, Small Science Developer, Boston Children's Museum. Sheila Terens and Sylvia Webb of School Number Four also participated in the Curriculum Development meeting. Special thanks also to George Tokieda, who in addition to his participation in the Curriculum Development meeting, conducted three very exciting inservice sessions for teachers at School Number Four.

Several people read and critiqued the manuscript for this guide, and we want to express our appreciation for their efforts. Thanks to Linda Colón, Administrator, Educational Equity Concepts; Mercedes Flores, Project S.E.E. (Sex Equity in Education), California State Department of Education; Pat Gray, Prekindergarten Director, School Number Four; Ellen Rubin, Special Education Staff Specialist, Educational Equity Concepts; and Sherri Shapiro, Frank Small, and Sylvia Webb, pilot testing teachers at School Number Four.

Special thanks go to Jim Anderson for graphic design of the book, to Mary Allison who copyedited the manuscript, Joni Miller for typing many drafts, and Ann Chwatsky and Ann-Marie Mott who took the photographs.

Finally, we wish to acknowledge that Beginning Math and Science Equitably was made possible by a grant from the Women's Educational Equity Act Program, U.S. Department of Education. We especially want to thank our Program Officer, John Fiegel, for encouragement and support throughout the Project.

CONTENTS

WHAT WILL HAPPEN IF...

PREFACE

What Will Happen If . . . Young Children and the Scientific Method is based on the premise that activities designed to develop math and science skills and an understanding of the role of technology are as essential to the early childhood curriculum as are activities to promote language development and prereading skills. If children are to gain an understanding of the world in which they live, attention must be paid to the scientific and technological aspects of that world from the beginning of the educational experience.

This guide will help teachers incorporate math, science, and technology-related activities into the daily life of the classroom in age-appropriate ways. The activities focus on the physical sciences rather than on the biological and ecological sciences that traditionally make up the early childhood science curriculum. With the help of this guide, you will be able to ensure that all children, regardless of sex, race, or disability, develop essential math and science skills.

HISTORY OF BEGINNING MATH AND SCIENCE EQUITABLY

Beginning Math and Science Equitably is a project of Educational Equity Concepts, Inc., a national, nonprofit organization founded in 1982 to develop programs and materials free of sex, race, and disability bias. The project was funded by a one-year grant from the U.S. Department of Education, Women's Educational Equity Act Program to develop, pilot test, produce, and disseminate an early childhood math and science curriculum guide with an equity approach.

The guide, *What Will Happen If . . . Young Children and the Scientific Method,* emphasizes visual-spatial and problem-solving activities. It provides strategies to ensure that all children, regardless of sex, race, or disability, begin to develop essential skills in the areas of math and science from the very beginning of their educational experience. The project was divided into three phases: curriculum planning and development, pilot testing, and production of a curriculum guide.

CURRICULUM PLANNING AND DEVELOPMENT

In January 1984, a diverse group of educators from across the country assembled in Educational Equity Concepts' New York headquarters for a two-day meeting to develop the thrust of the curriculum. Included in the group were teachers; administrators; researchers; equity specialists in the areas of sex, race, and disability; curriculum developers; and computer experts. In all, more than twenty people from the Northeast, the Midwest, and Canada participated.

For two days participants met in large and small groups to brainstorm ideas and then refine them into an overall curriculum design. Subject areas of the small groups were math, science, and technology. The math group speculated about what would happen if children didn't always have to come up with a quick and "correct" answer and instead were allowed to ruminate about numbers as mathematicians do. The science group experimented with hands-on materials — they made and swung pendulums, they cooked in a box-oven lined with aluminum foil and powered by a 40-watt bulb — and they discussed opportunities for creating physical science activities out of the everyday environment of the early childhood classroom. The technology group talked about the importance of fitting computers into a larger context of technology and became excited about providing children and teachers with the opportunity to "tinker" with machines — to take things apart without necessarily having to put them together again. The curriculum development meeting was challenging, stimulating, and fun and, in the course of the two days, the basic principles of the curriculum were defined:

- There is no need to create a distinction between math and science activities. Mathematics is defined as the science of numbers, and most scientific endeavors require knowledge and use of mathematical concepts. Therefore, it is beneficial for children to understand the interrelatedness of math and science from the beginning of their education.

- Science and math experiences are everywhere. They can be found within the classroom environment.

- The scientific method has an appropriate place in the early childhood classroom. It helps to systematize children's natural inclinations to experiment, observe, and discuss what they learn.

- Computers should be included in the larger context of technology. Classroom exploration and neighborhood trips can help children understand how technology (use of tools and machines) extends human ability.

- Activities are needed that focus on the physical sciences in addition to the more common preschool areas of biology and ecology.

The culmination of the curriculum planning and development phase of the project was taking the ideas generated by the curriculum development meeting and incorporating them into a series of math/science activities for children at the preschool, kindergarten, and first-grade levels.

PILOT TESTING

Pilot testing of Beginning Math and Science Equitably took place at School Number Four, the Early Childhood Center of the Lawrence (New York) Public Schools. The pilot site, in a nearby suburb of New York City, was unique in several ways: it drew 400 children from a five-town area into one early childhood center comprised of six preschool and thirteen all-day kindergarten classes; its population was racially and ethnically diverse and included Black, Hispanic, Chinese, Japanese, Korean, Italian, Jewish, and other children; and the socioeconomic range was from low-income to upper middle-income families. In addtion, the center had an unusually high quality teaching and administrative staff, and its educational program was excellent.

Prior to pilot testing the curricular activites at School Number Four, an inservice course was offered to early childhood teachers (pre k-third grade) throughout the district. Initially, four sessions were scheduled, including a general introduction to issues of nonsexist education, "tinkering" with small machines, and developing strategies for introducing technology into the curriculum. At the request of the teachers, three additional sessions were conducted with a science specialist and consisted of practical, hands-on science experiences. During these sessions teachers confronted their reluctance to touch materials generally considered "unpleasant" by working with snails, squid, and fish; performed experiments; and discussed and recorded their hypotheses and observations.

During the inservice period, three teachers volunteered to pilot test activities in their classrooms. A preschool teacher of four-year-olds agreed to pilot test sieves, water, and sand activities; a kindergarten teacher agreed to pilot test small machines and technology activities; and another kindergarten teacher agreed to pilot test physics activities using blocks, balls, and ramps.

In addition, School Number Four had a "science museum" and a part-time science specialist. All the kindergarten classes spent two sessions per week in the science museum during which half the children worked with the science specialist in one area of the room while the other half of the class did special activities with their teacher in another area of the room. Teachers agreed to pilot test some liquid-in-motion activities in the science museum with those children who were not working with the science specialist. Over the course of three weeks all the kindergartners had an opportunity to participate in the liquid-in-motion curriculum.

A project staff member was present at each of the liquid-in-motion sessions in the science museum. In some cases, the teacher conducted the activity and the staff person facilitated. In other cases, the process was reversed. This flexibility was based on the preference of the participating teacher.

The pilot testing of activities in the three classrooms took place over a five-week period. Initially, each of the classes received some posters and other resources to create a science atmosphere in their room, and the children were introduced to the concept of who can be a scientist and what a scientist does. The resources were chosen especially for their equity content.

After the introductory activities, each teacher pilot tested the activities specifically designed for her or his classroom. Each time a new activity was introduced, a project staff person was present to facilitate the process and to observe the results. After each new activity, teachers and project staff met briefly to share feedback, discuss problems, and plan for the follow-up. The teachers then continued to carry out the activity until every child in the group had participated.

THE GUIDE

This guide, *What Will Happen If . . . Young Children and the Scientific Method,* is the result of the work of Beginning Math and Science Equitably. It incorporates the curriculum ideas and philosophical approach to math and science developed by the diverse group of experts who met together at the project's inception. It also incorporates insights and first-hand experiences gained from teachers and administrators at School Number Four.

What Will Happen If . . . seeks to extend the early childhood curriculum in new ways by taking traditional materials and using them in age-appropriate math and science activities. Such activities foster the development of visual-spatial, problem-solving, and other math and science skills that are the building blocks of later achievement in these areas. It focuses on the physical sciences and on helping young children understand technology in the context of their daily lives. Above all, the guide has built into each activity ways to ensure that *all* children participate equally. Equal access to all areas of the curriculum from the beginning of the educational process is the right of every child regardless of sex, race, or disability.

INTRODUCTION

_____
_____
_____
_____
_____
_____
_____
_____
_____
_____
_____
_____

EARLY CHILDHOOD MATH AND SCIENCE – THE EQUITY ISSUES

The scientific method in the early childhood classroom? Five-year-old "scientists" engaged in physics experiments? Four-year-olds and five-year-olds predicting, observing, and documenting their findings? "Required" activities for preschoolers and kindergartners? Early childhood teachers eagerly planning and implementing science activities?

While all of this may sound a bit improbable, it is, in fact, what happened as a result of Beginning Math and Science Equitably, an early childhood program of Educational Equity Concepts, Inc., funded by the U.S. Department of Education, Women's Educational Equity Act Program. The overall goal of the project was to begin at the preschool level to strengthen the math and science curriculum for *all* children and to ensure the development of skills necessary for later achievement in these areas.

What is the need for such a project? First, if children are to understand the world they live in, they must, from the beginning of their education, be helped to develop skills in the areas of math and science. Today's children are born into an age of technological revolution, and they will become adults in the twenty-first century. Certainly by then, to participate in society as informed and productive citizens, knowledge of these fields will be essential for pursuing a broad range of careers, for making informed decisions, and for gathering and processing information.

Second, steps must be taken to ensure that all children regardless of sex, race, or disability have the opportunity to develop these skills. If past patterns are perpetuated, for the most part only white, male, nondisabled children will be encouraged to learn these skills that bring access to career advancement, decision making, and power.

Third, early childhood educators need to understand the important role they play both in terms of helping children understand the world they live in and in terms of the equity issues discussed above. Teachers of young children must be active in seeing that math and science skills are developed. They need to take conscious steps to ensure that all children have has the opportunity to participate in age-appropriate activities that foster skills and that provide familiarity and comfort with the technological aspects of the world they live in.

For at least a decade, teachers of young children consciously have tried to break down stereotypes regarding sex, race, and disability in many areas of their program, e.g., the use of certain play areas by sex-segregated groups, in interpersonal relationships between the sexes and between different racial and ethnic groups, and in bringing children with disabilities into mainstreamed settings. This same equity consciousness now needs to be applied to the math/science areas of the curriculum where biased societal attitudes based on commonly held perceptions rather than proven facts still prevail.

For example, one myth is that boys have more natural ability than girls for math and science. The fact is that the case for ''innate'' sex differences is not strong and, in the elementary grades, girls generally do better than boys in math.[1] Another myth is that girls don't like ''yucky'' activities like science. The fact is that girls are more likely than boys to model their teacher's behavior. Therefore, if a female teacher conveys that a science activity such as touching a snake or snail is ''unpleasant,'' girls are likely to accept this attitude and make it their own.[2]

Adult attitudes that may lead to avoidance of math and science activities altogether or relegate them to a minor role in the early childhood curriculum can be as limiting to children's development as any other form of bias. At the preschool level, a typical attitude is that science and math activities are less important than activities that foster reading and writing skills. In fact, it is equally important to begin early to incorporate math and science into the curriculum if children are to grow with proficiency and comfort in these areas.

THE EQUITY FOCUS – RESEARCH BACKGROUND

Beginning Math and Science Equitably is a response to two major areas of research. The first examines the lack of participation of women and people of color of both sexes in careers in math, science, and technology. The second looks at the sex-differentiated learning attributes and play patterns of girls and boys entering preschool and also examines how the structure of the typical early childhood classroom often exacerbates these differences.

Participation in Math, Science, and Technology

Turning to the first area of research, by the late 1970s:

- Of the nation's 2.7 million scientists, only 5 percent were female and 1.5 percent were Black;

- Men held 87 percent of the jobs in math, computers, and the life sciences and 99 percent of the jobs in engineering.[3]

The ramifications of these appalling statistics are doubly disturbing. They are troubling, first, in terms of the future employment and career development of girls and children of color of both sexes; and second, in terms of the minimal role that women and people of color without sufficient background can expect to play in determining the environmental, health, and energy future of this country.

In examining the root causes of deficits in the areas of math, science, and technology, researchers point to sex and race stereotyping, economic factors, cultural expectations, and poor teaching as contributing factors.[4] Although the literature doesn't include an analysis of the lack of participation by people with disabilities in careers in math and science, one can infer that similar contributing factors apply. Holly Knox, a noted equity specialist, places responsibility squarely on the shoulders of parents and educators:

> As parents and educators we have allowed — even aided and abetted — our female and minority youths to avoid the educational experiences that form essential building blocks for scientific and technical training. We've fed the myth that science and math are male domains and the property of the white middle class at that.[5]

Lucy Sells, in a now classic study, refers to how the lack of high school training in higher mathematics becomes a "critical filter" for keeping young women out of college level math and science programs. She points out that these are the very programs that lead to increased career options in fields of technology, architecture, landscape architecture, science, mathematics, business, and many others.[6] Patterns of avoidance combine with societal expectations and indifference to exclude girls from even considering, never mind preparing for, careers that require math, science, and technological training backgrounds. Again, one can infer that the same "critical filter" applies to children of color and children with disabilities.

Sex Differences in the Early Childhood Classroom

How does this process begin? By the time they enter preschool, girls and boys already have been socialized in very different ways by their parents and through messages from the larger community. Studies show that girls stay closer to parents and that boys explore their environment, roam further away from their parents, and become more independent.[7] Toys, too, are sex-differentiated. Boys tend to be given moving toys and building toys that develop large motor and visual-spatial skills, while girls typically receive dolls, art materials, and cleaning apparatus that develop small motor and social skills.

Selma Greenberg, a noted teacher educator and equity specialist, has organized this research into eight sets of learning attributes commonly observed in young children. Dr. Greenberg states that girls enter preschool with verbal, small muscular, repetitive, nurturing, one-to-one, role rehearsal, adult modeling, and impulse control experiences. Boys enter school with spatial, large muscular, inventive, managing, group, career and life options, direct instruction, and self-worth experiences.[8]

Dr. Greenberg goes on to state that once children enter preschool, they tend to self-select activities they already do well or can master with certainty. Once these activities are selected, children tend to continue to develop greater skill in the selected area. This can lead to learning deficits in the unselected areas for both girls and boys.[9]

Lisa Serbin, early childhood researcher, also has looked at patterns of sex-differentiated play in preschool. In research focusing on the specific visual-spatial skills that one learns by playing with blocks and other three-dimensional building and play activities, Dr. Serbin and her colleagues have found that "practice" can make a difference. First, they found that children of both sexes who played with male-preferred toys, e.g., blocks, transportation toys, and construction materials, showed relatively higher visual-spatial abilities then children of both sexes who played with female-preferred toys, e.g., dolls, housekeeping, and fine motor toys.

Next, to further test their hypothesis that play with traditionally male-preferred toys actually fosters the development of visual-spatial skills in young children, Dr. Serbin and her colleagues conducted a study to test the direct effect of this practice. Groups of preschoolers who received nine structured fifteen-minute lessons with three-dimensional construction materials over a five-week period did better on visual-spatial tests than children who participated only in the regular classroom curriculum.[10]

THE EARLY CHILDHOOD ENVIRONMENT AND SELF-SELECTION – IMPLICATIONS

The early childhood classroom both remediates and exacerbates the self-selection process that leads children into deficit areas of learning. To understand how and why this happens, one must look at early childhood education and the structure of the typical preschool day.

Most early childhood teachers are taught to set up a rich learning environment comprised of areas for dramatic play, "housekeeping," blocks, manipulative materials, books, records, art work, and water or sand play. Time also is scheduled for outdoor play, and many programs have a science area and/or animals to care for. The curriculum and materials are designed to develop cognitive, social, and emotional skills needed for success later in more formal academic settings. Although these skills are offered to children through informal activities and games, the antecedents of mathematics and sciences, social studies, language arts, creative arts, and athletics are all present. Within the curriculum framework, however, the typical pattern is to let children self-select most activities according to personal preferences.

There are some areas of the curriculum that are "required." Most programs have a story or circle time to foster listening and discussion skills. Others have a scheduled snack or meal time during which, in addition to eating nutritional foods, children are encouraged to develop verbal and social skills. Many programs have structured activities centered around reading readiness — small muscle, verbal, and eye/hand coordination skills development. In other words, structured and "required" activities are those that remediate boys' learning deficits because they are in the areas that are deemed important for preparing children for the prime elementary school tasks, namely reading and writing.[11]

The same attention, however, is not paid to girls' deficit areas — the development of large motor, visual-spatial, and problem-solving skills. Activities that foster these skills generally are relegated to the "free-play" segments of the curriculum. For example, during work time, children are free to select blocks or trucks, but in most cases they are not required to do so. Similarly, everyone may be required to spend some time outdoors, but once there, each child is free to choose her or his own activity. Consequently, many girls continue to play house or work with sand, rather than using the outdoors for spatial exploration or large motor activities.

Looking at the areas in which girls and boys typically self-select brings one face-to-face with the equity issues. Boys' areas are those that help to develop visual-spatial, problem-solving, and allied skills that often contribute to later academic and career choices in mathematics, science, technology, and skilled trades, areas of high status and power within the larger society.

In contrast, girls' preferred areas are those that help to develop social and verbal skills and small-motor coordination that often contribute to later academic and career choices in the humanities, the helping professions, support services, and full-time homemaking, areas that are allotted low status and little or no power by the larger society.[12]

Of course, no one is suggesting that early childhood educators consciously set up unequal situations for children. The individual approach and the rich and varied activities of most programs make them exciting learning environments. Like most fields, however, early childhood education needs to be willing to reexamine established practices in the light of new research. Families and schools are still socializing and educating children in sex-differentiated modes that are neither in tune with the realities of today nor are preparatory for the world they will experience as adults.

TEACHERS AND TECHNOLOGY

Dr. Jessie Bernard, the reknowned sociologist, has described women as "immigrants in the world of technology."[13] Dr. Selma Greenberg describes the same concept with an amusing, but all too true, observation:

> Scene One:
> A man drives into a service station to get gas and to have the oil, water, and battery checked. He jumps out of the car, peers under the hood, and checks the oil gauge when the attendant tells him he needs oil. He asks questions, acts as if he knows what's going on, and learns a few things in the process.

> Scene Two:
> A women drives into the same station for the same services. She sits patiently in the car while the gas station attendant pumps the gas, checks the oil, battery, and water; tells her she needs oil; and proceeds to put in a quart. He finishes, tells her how much she owes, she pays and drives off.

While more and more women now pump gas, fix cars, and change their own oil, one would have to agree that scene two above still describes the majority of women.

Women use technology, and they do fix things. Women regularly use and fix household appliances, toys, and school-related machines such as projectors and mimeographs. The machines they use and fix, however, are those that are relegated to low status and are considered unimportant by the larger society.

This was not always the case. In preindustrial times both women's and men's tasks were seen as essential to the survival of the family. The tools and technology needed for farm life were not as divergent in status as home-based and industrial tools and technology later became. As men moved further away from the home site to perform their work, machinery acquired a new mystique and importance understood only by other men. As a result, the development of new forms of technology, especially since the end of World War II, has become male identified and dominated. For a long time women have been discouraged from understanding or participating in the technological revolution. It wasn't considered ''feminine'' to be good in math and science or to have an interest in machines and technology.

Of course, some women overcame the barriers placed before them and, despite the odds, pursued careers in math, science, and technology. One can, however, easily understand why the majority of women are uneasy and insecure about their abilities in these areas.

This uneasiness and insecurity is quite apparent when talking to preschool teachers, most of whom are women. In fact, many teachers of young children cite the fact that one needs little or no background in math or science as one factor in choosing to teach at the early childhood or elementary level. And, if one's inclination is to avoid math and science activities altogether, or give them a minor place in the curriculum, children will understand that message, whether or not it is articulated.

It is crucial to remember that, except for family members, teachers are the most important role models for young children. Children quickly adopt patterns of speech, favorite words and expressions, and reflect their teacher's attitudes, both positive or negative. Girls especially tend to stay physically closer and to model behavior after their teacher. For example, if a teacher acts cold and uncomfortable outdoors, some children, again almost always girls, will take the cue and not enjoy outdoor play. Conversely, if a teacher models enjoyment of vigorous outdoor play by running and jumping, these same girls will be more likely to use the outdoors to full advantage for large motor development.

The same analogy holds for curriculum activities related to math, science, and technology. If a teacher is indifferent to, or avoids these subjects, only the most interested children will pursue such activities. If, on a field trip, a teacher is reluctant to let children explore ideas with which she or he is unfamiliar or uncomfortable — for example, how does the hose on a fire engine work or what makes the computerized banking machine dispense money? — only the most curious children will find someone who can explain these "mysteries" to them. The children who most need to explore in these areas will not pursue them unless a conscious effort is made.

How can early childhood teachers make themselves comfortable enough with math, science, and technology activities to undertake them with children? For at least part of the answer, it is useful to think about how young children learn. They learn through their own activity — by direct hands-on experience. As adults we may not approach new areas of learning with the willing minds of children. If, however, one is committed to the importance of providing children with opportunities for exploration, one can take the first step by seeking out new experiences in the math, science and technological areas. For example, when arranging a walk to the bank, take an advance trip by yourself and ask a bank employee to explain how the money machine works. You then have time to process the information before translating it into age-appropriate language to answer children's questions. This is worth the extra time, since anxiety is lessened by familiarity with the subject.

Another aspect to becoming comfortable with less familiar topics is to realize that you may know more than you think you do. Early childhood teachers need to validate for themselves (and for each other) what they *do know* about math, science, and technology. Is there something you learned in a high school or college chemistry course that would translate into a new and different science activity? Could you redesign a cooking activity with a scientific focus?

Peer support also can play a role in overcoming anxiety. Some people on staff may openly (or secretly) enjoy machines, or math, or science. They can model for others how to approach these areas with children. Or teams of teachers — one who is comfortable with math, science and technology and one who is not — can work together on activities.

While some early childhood teachers may choose the field because it doesn't require much knowledge of math and science, they also choose the field because they enjoy the challenge of working with young children and the hands-on, experiential approach to learning. Working with young children requires a person with an open mind, flexibility, and the ability to try new approaches. An early childhood educator takes a comprehensive approach to learning. She or he understands that if a child is to be allowed to develop her or his full potential, the social, emotional, physical, and cognitive needs of that child must be addressed. Such a person can meet the challenge of incorporating math, science, and technology into the early childhood curriculum.

ABOUT THIS GUIDE

What Will Happen If . . . Young Children and the Scientific Method follows several basic principles decided upon by the diverse group of experts who participated in the curriculum development meeting at the beginning of the project (see "History of Beginning Math and Science Equitably"). One of those principles is that, since the fields of math and science are thoroughly interrelated, activities need not be rigidly divided into one area or the other, but can and should contain elements of both. For example, when children construct block ramps to explore the effects of inclined planes on speed and distance — a physics concept — they learn math skills as they predict how far a ball will roll and count the number of blocks used to make ramps of different heights.

Each of the activities in this guide fosters the development of the visual-spatial and problem-solving skills considered vital to later achievement in math and science. In the best tradition of early childhood education, the activities also foster the development of vocabulary, verbal, observation, recording, and other interdisciplinary skills. Technology is introduced to children in the context of the world around them. Machines are introduced as tools that can extend human capacity — in the home, in the school, and in the larger community — and computers are introduced within the same context.

Another basic principle of this guide is to develop math and science activities from traditional areas of the early childhood curriculum — blocks, water and sand, outdoor play, and trips — and to apply the scientific method to each activity. Therefore, instructional computer activities involving the use of commercial software are not included. If readers of this guide are using computers with young children, it is recommended that the spirit of inquiry and the focus on equitable access that is an essential part of this curriculum be extended to use of computers as well.

CONCLUSIONS

The preceding pages have asked early childhood educators to reexamine some basic early childhood tenets in the light of new aspects of educational equity. As the recent findings of the High Scope Perry Project document, early childhood education can have a positive, long-term impact and help children to achieve more in school and in their adult lives.[14] Early childhood education can limit children's potential by perpetuating sex-differentiated play patterns that can lead to areas of deficit for both girls and boys. It also can expand children's potential by discouraging sex differences and by taking positive steps to redress deficit areas of learning for all children.

The challenge for educators begins in the preschool. If we are to achieve educational equity, the deficit areas of all children must be addressed. Required activities to develop preformal math and science skills need to be structured into the daily program along with those that already are required for the development of preformal reading and writing skills.

What Will Happen If . . . Young Children and the Scientific Method was written to help early childhood educators meet this challenge. The activities in this guide are designed to foster early math and science skills, to help children understand technology in the world around them, and to ensure that *all* children, not just the few who self-select, participate.

NOTES

1. Sells, Lucy W. "Mathematics — A Critical Filter," *The Science Teacher,* Vol. 45, No. 2, Feb. 1978.

2. Serbin, Lisa A. and Burchardt, Carol J. "Sex-stereotyped Play Behavior in the Preschool Classroom: Effects of Teacher Presence and Modeling." Paper presented to Society for Research and Child Development, New Orleans, LA, March, 1977.

3. Knox, Holly. "Math and Science Improvements Must Involve Female and Minority Students," *Education Week,* May 11, 1983, p. 24.

4. Berryman, Susan E. *Who Will Do Science?* New York: Rockefeller Foundation, Nov. 1983.

5. Knox, Holly. op. cit.

6. Sells, Lucy W. op. cit.

7. Goldberg, Susan and Lewis, Michael. "Play Behavior in the Year-Old Infant: Early Sex Differences." *Child Development* 40, 1969: 21-31. And Saegert, Susan and Hart, Roger A. "The Development of Sex Differences on the Environmental Competence of Children." In *Women in Society,* ed. P. Burnett, Chicago: Maaroufa Press, 1976.

8. Greenberg, Selma. "Educational Equity in Early Childhood Environments." In *Handbook for Achieving Sex Equity Through Education,* edited by Susan S. Klein. Baltimore and London: The Johns Hopkins University Press, 1985.

9. Ibid.

10. Serbin, Lisa. "Play Activities and the Development of Visual-Spatial Skills," *Equal Play,* Vol. 1, No. 4, Fall 1980.

11. Greenberg, Selma. op. cit.

12. Berryman, Susan E., op. cit., 105.

13. Bernard, Jessie. *The Female World.* New York: Free Press (Division of Macmillan), 1981.

14. Perry Preschool Program. *Changed Lives.* Ypsilanti, MI: High Scope Educational Research Foundation, 1984.

USING THE SCIENTIFIC METHOD WITH YOUNG CHILDREN

How to Do It

EXPANDING MATH AND SCIENCE IN THE CURRICULUM

The title, *What Will Happen If . . .* , is taken from the question that is the core of the activities throughout this guide. The question is designed to expand children's thinking, to encourage them to explore the world around them in new ways. By asking the question, you convey to children that learning is not a series of rote answers, but a process of thinking and experimenting. It is active not passive, creative not mechanical, and, as the teachers who pilot tested the activities found out, exciting, challenging, and fun.

The activities in *What Will Happen If . . .* foster visual-spatial and problem-solving skills and help children understand and appreciate the role of technology in the world around them. The focus is on the physical sciences, rather than the more traditional ones of biology and ecology.

By applying a simplified version of the scientific method, familiar components of the early childhood classroom are expanded to explore mathematic and scientific concepts in age-appropriate ways. For example, in "Water and Sand," children make and use sieves to explore the concept of flow. In "Bottles and Liquids," children use their senses to collect "data" and to explore the concepts of density and viscosity. In "Blocks," children build ramps to explore momentum and extrapolate data from their findings.

In addition, the guide takes technology, a component that is not usually found in the early childhood curriculum, and helps teachers to make it familiar. In "Machines and Me: Technology in the Early Childhood Classroom," children learn about machines, computers, and technology in general by making books and collages, going on trips, and by taking things apart and putting them back together.

The activities are not designed as one-shot experiments. Instead, they are part of an overall approach that incorporates a systematic, creative thinking process into the existing curriculum. This approach can be applied to all areas of the curriculum. Activities that develop preformal reading and writing skills are already built into the curriculum on a daily basis. Visual-spatial and problem-solving skills need this same attention so that children can develop them as they do all skills — slowly and over time.

FORMAT OF GUIDE

The *What Will Happen If* . . . curriculum begins with a "Preliminary Activity: Creating a 'What Scientist Do' Collage," which, without fancy or expensive new equipment, helps to create a receptive atmosphere for the activities that follow. There are four overall areas of exploration:

- Water and Sand: Using Sieves to Expore the Concept of Flow;

- Blocks: Exploring Momentum with Ramps and Balls;

- Bottles and Liquids: Exploring Solubility, Density, and Viscosity;

- Machines and Me: Technology in the Early Childhood Classroom.

Each chapter begins with an *Overview* that highlights how the scientific method extends that area of early childhood learning and discusses the equity issues inherent in the exploration of that particular concept. The *Overview* is followed by two or more step-by-step activities that build from simple to more complex. Each activity is organized into the following sections: *Purpose, What Children Learn, Format, Materials and Supplies, Background Information, Acitivity, Equity Issues, Be Aware,* and *Extensions. Background Information* provides a simple explanation of the mathematic and scientific principles involved so that they can be translated into words young children will understand. The *Equity Issues* call attention to the ways in which teachers can assure that all children participate equally, and *Be Aware* points out possible pitfalls and how to avoid them. *Extensions* illustrate how the basic concepts can be used in other situations. Everything is based on first-hand experiences and observations from the Beginning Math and Science Equitably pilot testing.

The activities are designed for use with children ages four, five, and six. But, as with every activity, you need to assess your children's abilities beforehand, While the activities have been written with an easy-to-use, step-by-step approach, they are not meant to be cookbook recipes. For example, the time allotted for each activity is meant only to be a guideline. An underlying principle of this guide is that children need time to explore myriad possibilities in both math and science and that the pressure to come up with a "correct" answer often stifles such exploration. Therefore, in doing the experiments, use more or less time according to the needs of your group.

Every classroom situation is unique, and every child's learning mode is her or his own. Read through the activities before you begin to use them. They will be most effective if you adapt them to your particular style of teaching.

WHAT IS THE SCIENTIFIC METHOD?

The scientific method is a system of investigation that typically involves a variety of steps, beginning with a statement of a question or problem and a prediction of the answer (or hypothesis). An experiment is then conducted to test the prediction (or hypothesis). The observation of the experiment leads to the generation of conclusions and the documentation of the results.

While this seems like heavy-duty learning for four-, five-, and six-year-olds, in fact, it is a process that children take to easily. It builds upon children's natural desire for exploration and curiosity to find out how things work. It is a method of learning that gives children a structure for their exploration and helps them to formulate and articulate their ideas, sharpen their observation skills, and communicate the results to others.

For the purposes of the activities in this guide and for working with young children, once a problem has been posed, the scientific method has been broken down into the following steps: *predicting* (or, in a young child's words, guessing) what will happen, *conducting* (or doing) *the experiment, observing* (or looking at) what actually happens, *making conclusions* about (or discussing) the results, and *documenting* (or writing down) the results. This process, followed by a group discussion of what happened, may lead to further questions and experimentation.

_____

_____

_____

_____

_____

TURNING FAMILIAR ACTIVITIES INTO EXPERIMENTS

In addition to the specific activities outlined in this guide, the opportunity for scientific learning is present in just about every classroom activity. Stop a minute and think about your daily routine. Think about the difference if, before a familiar activity such as cleaning up the art table, you asked children *"What will happen if . . . ?"* *"What will happen if* you clean up the clay on the table with a dry sponge?" *"What will happen if* you clean up the clay on the table with a very wet sponge?" *"What will happen if* the colors of the paints mix together?"

Once you ask the question, it sets the remaining steps of the scientific method in motion. For example, undoubtedly in exploring the properties of water, you have had children take two cups of water and put one in the freezer and one on the classroom shelf to see what happens. Just think how much richer the experience could be if you asked children, *"What will happen if* you put one cup of water in the freezer, one cup of water on the refrigerator shelf, and one cup of water on a table in the classroom?" Ask the children to predict what will happen and write their predictions on a large sheet of paper. Then have the children conduct the experiment. The next day, ask children to observe, discuss their findings, and draw some conclusions about what happened and why. Children then can document their findings by making an experience chart about their experiment. Following the documentation, further discussion can lead to other generalizations and questions.

THE IMPORTANCE OF DOCUMENTATION

Documentation is an important ingredient of all the activities in this guide. Through documentation, children learn how to write down what they have observed and concluded. This provides a permanent record for children to refer back to, and it enables children to talk to others and share what they have learned.

There are many kinds of documentation. Some, like writing down a recipe or making an experience chart, you may already do but not think of as documentation. Others are more sophisticated, like the data dot charts in the "Blocks" activities. For these, children record the results of their experiment by using different colored stick-on dots. These charts not only document the experiment, but provide the means for children to begin to "read statistics" and learn how to extrapolate data from their own findings.

THE PURPOSE OF STRUCTURE

It is important to understand that a structured scientific activity is not inconsistent with creativity and exploration. In fact, the very nature of the scientific method is to encourage children to think creatively and to explore all possibilities. Imagination is an important part of forming hypotheses. Since it is an experiment, however, the exploration must be done within certain rules to ensure reliability and validity.

For an experiment to be reliable, it has to be set up identically from one time to another, so that each time it is conducted, the results will be the same. In the same way, for an experiment to be valid, it has to be set up so that new variables aren't introduced that will mix up the results. For example, one of the "Bottles and Liquids" activities explores how fast an object travels through different kinds of liquids. Identical screws are placed in one bottle filled with water and one filled with light corn syrup. In this experiment, it is important not only that the screws be identical, but that the bottles be identical as well. Otherwise, if one tall and one short bottle were used, the screw might very well fall to the bottom of the shorter bottle faster, regardless of the liquid in it. Thus, the variable of the size of the bottles would confound the results.

These structured activities are not designed to replace informal play. During their regular play, children should be encouraged to use materials in many different ways. However, children should also understand that, while they are conducting an experiment, a structured set of rules apply.

Another aspect of structure is the required nature of the activities. Teachers found that it was quite easy, without being obtrusive, to make sure all children participated. As is discussed in the "Introduction," these activities are designed to strengthen the math and science curriculum for all children. Requiring children to participate assures that everyone has the opportunity to acquire the same skills. Children who have deficits in the area of math and science skills cannot choose to avoid the very activities they need to remedy those deficits. Required activities also help children who are hesitant to choose activities that are outside the role they perceive as "appropriate" — a role that can be defined by sex, race, or disability.

Another benefit of required activities is that they can help provide clues to some children's difficulties that would not be evident otherwise. For example, a five-year-old boy who was reading on a third-grade level, was assumed to be among the "brightest" in the class. His difficulty with some of the "Blocks" activities gave his teacher insight about this boy's need for additional work in the visual-spatial area.

THE ROLE OF THE TEACHER

For the activities in this guide, the teacher's role can best be described as facilitator of the learning process. Within the established structure of the scientific method mistakes can be made. Too often, children think of math and science as subjects that have "right" answers. Children need to be assured that making mistakes and learning from them is all part of mathematic and scientific exploration and an important part of the learning process.

This does not mean, however, that misinformation should be passed along. Children may come to inaccurate conclusions. As a teacher, you need to help them understand this, without giving them the impression that they have done something "wrong." To uncover why a child has come up with an inaccurate conclusion, you will need to go back, step-by-step, through the process. You might find that a child didn't know which liquid was water and which syrup, or didn't understand what farther or nearer meant, or that her or his attention had wandered during the experiment.

To be a facilitator, you need to know the steps of an experiment and to understand what is expected to happen. The background information in each activity will help with this, but as with children, the best way to learn is by doing. So, in all cases, it is suggested that you do the experiment yourself beforehand.

Despite advance preparation, however, an unforseen problem may occur as you work with the children on an experiment. Remember that if you want children to feel that mistakes are part of the process of inquiry, you need to be willing to make a mistake yourself. You are a role model for the children. If they see that you are comfortable about making a mistake, finding out what went wrong, remedying the problem, and proceeding with the experiment, children, in turn, will know that it is alright for them to do the same. As the children's role model, you will be able to create, by your attitudes and the way you approach and facilitate the activities, an atmosphere that says math and science are exciting and fun.

CREATING A SCIENTIFIC ENVIRONMENT FOR ALL CHILDREN

The activities in this guide will help you make your classroom reflect the science and math that is all around. They focus on the physical sciences, and they are structured to add new and different dimensions to your classroom teaching. They do not replace informal play, but they can revitalize it. They build children's visual-spatial and problem-solving skills, while helping them to see the aesthetic aspects of science. They help children become familiar with technology and require that all children, regardless of sex, race, or disability, participate.

As with all good education, you will be learning along with your children, so you could regard the activities as your learning experiences as well. Since some of the activities may not be part of your traditional curriculum, at first you may not feel totally comfortable with them. But, as the teachers found out in the pilot testing, any initial reluctance on your part will be overcome by the children's enthusiasm and exuberance.

PRELIMINARY ACTIVITY

Creating a "What Scientists Do" Collage

OVERVIEW

The types of materials and resources that you select for your classroom give children clear messages about what should and should not be of interest to them. To help children develop an interest in math and science, you do not have to buy expensive equipment. You can begin simply by including science- and math-related materials as a part of your everyday classroom resources.

Making a "What Scientists Do" collage is a natural way to begin. The collage will help to set the stage for the activities that follow. It provides a jumping off point for discussions of what science is and the variety of work that scientists do. It also can create a receptive atmosphere for an introduction to the scientific method.

It is important that all children feel they belong in this science- and math-related atmosphere. You can help by making sure that the pictures available for your collage represent a variety of adults and children engaged in a broad range of science- and math-related work. By including women as well as men, girls as well as boys, people of color, and people who are disabled, you will be beginning math and science equitably for all the children in your classroom.

ACTIVITY

PURPOSES
- To create an atmosphere that encourages all children to be interested in mathematical and scientific pursuits.
- To have children make a "What Scientists Do" collage that is nonsexist, multiracial, and includes people who are disabled.
- To help children understand the scientific method.
- To help children learn about what scientists do.
- To incorporate science- and math-related resources into the general classroom environment.

WHAT CHILDREN LEARN

- About the work of scientists.
- That disabled and nondisabled women and men from all racial and ethnic backgrounds can be scientists.
- New vocabulary, e.g., scientist, experiment, predict, document.

FORMAT

A. Large group discussion (5-10 minutes).
B. Small group activity.

MATERIALS AND SUPPLIES

Experience chart paper and markers

Large paper for collage

Glue

Scissors

Pictures of scientists at work (adults and children)
Pictures of adults and children can be collected from science magazines such as *Discover, Omni, Scientific American, Popular Mechanics, National Geographic, World, Science and Children, 3-2-1 Contact,* and *Enter.* For additional suggestions, see "Resources."

BACKGROUND INFORMATION

According to the *American Heritage School Dictionary,* "science" is defined as "The study and theoretical explanation of natural phenomena" and "Any systematic activity requiring study and method." While there are many definitions of science, for children, a simple explanation would be best, e.g., "Science is finding out about things around us."

A scientist, then, is a person who is curious, likes to try out ideas, and studies the things around us. For example, a botanist studies plants, a geologist studies rocks, a paleontologist studies fossils, a zoologist studies animals, and so forth. Since the activities in this guide are based on the premise that science and math are inter-related, it is important to note that mathematics is the science of numbers — and a mathematician is a scientist who studies numbers.

A scientist also conducts experiments, and an experiment is the process of studying in an organized manner. For a description of this process — known as the scientific method — see "Using the Scientific Method with Young Children: How To Do It."

ACTIVITY

A. Large group discussion

1. During circle time, ask children, "What do you think science is?" "Does anyone know what scientists do?" Write children's responses on a sheet of experience chart paper. Discuss with children that science is the study of things around us and a scientist is a person who is curious, likes to try out ideas, and studies the things around us. Since children love learning new words that sound funny and interesting, you might talk about what it means to be a mathematician, a geologist, or paleontologist, or zoologist. Then add these new words to the experience chart.

2. Lay out the picture collection of scientists and have each child select one that she or he finds interesting. Ask all the children to talk about why they chose the pictures they did. Ask them to explain what the person in the picture is doing. As they describe what the person is doing, write their words on the experience chart paper. These could be as simple as "look," "think," "guess," or "stir things." At this point, you could add the words that describe the scientific method such as "experiment," "question," "predict," "conduct," "observe," "make conclusions," and "document." Explain them to children in words they will understand, e.g., "to predict is to guess what will happen" or "to document is to tell other people what you found."

3. After all children have talked about their pictures, write "What Scientists Do" on a large sheet of paper and tell children that they are going to use their pictures to make a collage about the work of scientists.

4. Ask children if they ever work like scientists. Help them to understand that they are all working like scientists when they try to figure out how things work. This would be a good opportunity to explain that you will be introducing some new activities and that they all are going to be able to do experiments and work like scientists as the year goes on.

B. Collage-making

During work time following the discussion, have children use their pictures to create a large "What Scientist Do" collage for the classroom. Have magazines or booklets available so children can cut out additional pictures as well. Hang up the "What

Scientists Do" collage and experience chart together at children's eye level.

EQUITY ISSUES

There are several equity issues to consider when collecting pictures for the "What Scientists Do" collage":

- Women should be portrayed performing a variety of science- and math-related tasks, including outdoors ones, and using heavy and complex equipment.

- Pictures should reflect diversity in terms of race and ethnicity.

- People who are disabled should be included.

- A broad range of jobs representing science and its applications should be included.

BE AWARE

Compiling an equitable picture collection of scientists at work might not be easy. Many sources still depict scientists predominently as white nondisabled males and perpetuate the notion of scientists as people in white coats in laboratory settings.

EXTENSIONS

The "What Scientists Do" collage is just the beginning of the creation of a science- and math- related environment. Other resources, such as posters and books, can be added to the classroom. While science- and math-related resources that are age-appropriate are not easy to find, there are some good materials available (see "Resources" for complete listing).

You also can take pictures of children doing science- and math-related activities in the classroom and add them to the collage or a general science display. Children can bring in photographs of their parents or other relatives who work in math, science, and technology fields and add them to the "What Scientists Do" collage.

In addition, science- and math-related items can be incorporated into the dramatic play area. Materials such as measuring tools, plastic test tubes, a magnifying glass, gyroscope, and so forth would convert the dramatic play area into a "scientist's workplace" for all children.

WATER AND SAND

Using Sieves to Explore the Concept of Flow

OVERVIEW

Water and sand play are basic and familiar components of the early childhood curriculum. Through activities such as pouring, sifting, siphoning, suctioning, rippling, and churning, children experience, in informal ways, essential math and science concepts such as comparison, conservation, and flow.

The activities that follow focus mainly on flow, which is a concept in the area of physics. Children compare the flow when their sieve is held higher or lower over the water. They are helped to observe the difference in flow between a large hole and a small hole, and they hear the different sounds water makes depending on the material of the sieve and its height from the water or sand. Later, they use their sieves in both water and sand to compare differences in the way water and sand flow through the same sieve.

As children pour water and sift sand, their play is structured according to the scientific method. Before they begin the activities, children make sieves, which are tools for conducting their experiment; then after a question is posed, children predict, conduct, observe, conclude, and, finally, document their findings. As they work, children talk to each other and respond to their teacher's questions that are designed to help them articulate and clarify what is happening. Children learn to think in new ways, build social skills, learn new vocabulary, and enjoy themselves. For example, when a group of four-year-olds worked with their sieves in water, they spontaneously exchanged sieves and, at the suggestion of their teacher, thought of many words that described the sounds the water was making as it flowed through the sieves. Soon, children began trying to catch the water by putting their sieves one underneath the other. Then, everyone in the small group caught on and they all put their sieves under each other creating a cascading fountain to the delight of everyone, adults and children included.

Structured activities such as these are not meant to replace informal play but rather to add a new and different dimension to water and sand activities. Teachers remarked that, in addition to extending math and science content, the activities were a catalyst for revitalizing regular water and sand play when it had become desultory and somewhat boring for the children.

Because the water and sand activities are required, girls and boys participate in them equally. Children who might not choose to work with hammers and nails do so when they make their sieves. This was illustrated graphically during the pilot testing when one girl, who initially was reluctant to participate in the activity, became so involved in the process of making holes in her sieve, she almost didn't make it to the water table! She had discovered that if she started a hole with a thin nail and then widened it with a thicker nail, she ended up with a smooth, well-rounded hole. Everytime she produced one of these fine holes, she hooked up and smiled broadly at the adult who was supervising the sieve-making.

The Water and Sand activities include:

Activity I   *Making and Using Sieves with Water and Sand*

Activity II   *Comparing How Water and Sand Flow Through Sieves*

ACTIVITY I

MAKING AND USING SIEVES WITH WATER

PURPOSES

- To help children gain familiarity with tools, e.g., hammers and nails.
- To provide children with the experience of making a sieve.
- To help children explore different ways water can flow through a sieve.
- To help children organize and document information.

WHAT CHILDREN LEARN

- How to use a hammer and nails.
- How to make a sieve.
- How water flows through a sieve.
- Vocabulary, e.g., sieves, flow, drip, drop.
- Ways to document observations.
- Observation skills.
- Small motor coordination.
- Eye/hand coordination.

FORMAT

A. Large group discussion (5-10 minutes).
B. Small group activity.
   1. Making the sieves (15 minutes per group)
   2. Using the sieves in water (15-30 minutes per group)
C. Large group discussions (10-15 minutes each).

MATERIALS AND SUPPLIES

Containers
An assortment of plastic, foil, styrofoam, and wax containers, e.g.,
empty margarine, milk, and deli-counter containers; styrofoam take-
out food trays (at least 1½ inches deep); foil pie, loaf, or layer pans;
waxed cardboard buckets (hotel ice buckets).

Hammers

Thick and thin nails with large heads

Four blocks
two unit size and two half-unit size

Water table
or large basin around which three to four children can easily work

Food coloring (optional)

Smocks

Experience chart paper and marker

Waterproof marker

BACKGROUND INFORMATION

When the children are constructing the sieves, the amount of hammering needed to make the holes will depend on the material chosen.

For example, a plastic deli-container requires more force than a foil pan. For a styrofoam take-out container it is sufficient to use the nails to punch the holes; no hammer is needed.

The rate and ease with which water will flow through the sieves will depend on how much friction or resistance it meets. The friction or resistance can be caused by the material of the container and the size and smoothness or roughness of the holes. The number of holes also will make a difference in the flow; naturally the more holes in the sieve, the more quickly water will flow through. The height at which children hold the sieve will have an effect on the splash, the ripples, and the bubbles formed in the water below. The higher the sieve is held, the more splash, ripples, and bubbles the flow will cause.

ACTIVITY

Start preparations for making the sieves about two weeks in advance. You either can ask children to bring in containers from home or collect them yourself. In any case, be sure to have a broad variety of size and shape containers make the experiment more interesting.

A. *Large group discussion*

Have a sample of each kind of container and a sieve, either hand-made or readymade, available. In a class meeting tell children that they are going to collect containers to make sieves. The children may already be familiar with sieves from playing in a sandbox at home or at the beach or at the sand table at school. Ask them to tell you everything they know about sieves and then hold up the sample. If the children are to bring in the containers from home, send a note informing parents about the experiments, carefully explaining the types of containers you will need. This is a positive way to increase home/school communication. If the children are bringing in the containers, allow a few days for collecting them. If you already have collected the containers yourself, tell the children that starting tomorrow each person in the class will make a sieve to use in water. Be sure to help the children understand that it may take a few days for everyone to make and use a sieve, but that everyone will have a turn.

If you already have made a "What Scientists Do" collage (see "Preliminary Activity"), you may want to remind children about it and tell them that they are going to work like scientists when they experiment with the sieves. If you have not yet introduced the words scientist and experiment and given a simple definition for each, you can do so at this time.

B. Small group activity

1. Making the sieves

a) Have a variety of containers on a table along with nails, hammers, and blocks. It is a good idea to cover the table with a layer of newspaper to avoid damage from the nails and to cushion the noise of hammering.

b) Choose three or four children to work together, making sure to strike a balance between girls and boys and more verbal and less verbal children.

c) Have the children turn the containers upside down and make holes using the different size nails. One good trick is to start a hole with a thin nail and enlarge it with a thicker one. This process makes for smoother holes. Another helpful hint is to put a block inside the container as a stabilizer. The size of the block will depend on the size of the container, and the block may have to be moved around to allow the nails to go through all parts of the container bottom. During the pilot testing, children often used the claw part of the hammer to extricate a nail if it got stuck in the plastic. Encourage the children to be creative about their patterns of holes. Some children may want many holes, some just a few. Variety will add interest to the activity. You will have to use your judgment about how independently the children can use the hammer and nails. Use a waterproof marker to write each child's name on her or his sieve.

d) As the children are making their sieves, pose questions that will encourage them to predict about how the sieves will work:

- *What will happen if* you put water into the sieve? Do you think the water will come out? How?
- Will the water make any sound?
- How do you think the water will look?

2. Using the sieves in water

a) As each small group finishes making sieves, have them move over to the water table or basin, roll up their sleeves, and put on smocks.

b) Have the water ready and, if possible, color it with a few drops of food coloring. Tell the children that now is the time to experiment with their sieves like scientists, finding out all the things that can happen when they put water through a sieve.

c) Let the children experiment freely for several minutes while you take notes on their observations. If it seems necessary, begin to ask questions to stimulate their observations:

- *What will happen if* all the sieves are at the same level?
- *What will happen if* we raise our sieves?
- *What will happen if* we use the sieves near the water?
- Through whose sieve is water flowing slowly? Why?
- Through whose sieve is water flowing fast? Why?
- How does the water sound as it flows out of the sieve?

d) When each child has used her or his sieve for a while, ask the children to exchange sieves for a few minutes before the activity is over.

e) After the children have experimented with the sieves for about fifteen minutes, ask them to tell you what they found out (use your own notes to jog their memories). Write down what they say in a "Sieves and Water" report. Encourage the use of vocabulary related to the scientific method, e.g., observe, experiment. Also encourage descriptive words. In the pilot testing of this activity, four-year-olds had great fun describing the look and sound of the water with words like drip, drop, dribble, and phrases like "sounds like the rain."

f) Repeat the process of making and using sieves and documenting the experience with a "Sieves and Water" report for each group until everyone in the class has participated.

C. *Large group discussion*

1. When everyone has had a turn working with the sieves, you will want the children to discuss their experiences together as a large group. You may want to let each child hold her or his sieve during the meeting, review the sieves and water experiences, and read each group's report to the whole class. Help children make comparisons of the reports noting what was alike and different. Bind the "Sieves and Water" reports into a book and place it in the class library.

EQUITY ISSUES

This activity involves working with tools, working with water, and analyzing and articulating the process. Most children, if left totally free to make their own choices, do not gravitate toward all these types of activities. For example, a girl might typically choose water play, but might not choose to work with hammer and nails, while a boy might typically choose workbench activities, but not participate in writing a report. Therefore, by requiring that everyone participate, children are equitably exposed to a wide range of skills. Also, by thinking about equity issues when choosing children for the small groups, the teacher has an opportunity to structure the activity so that it has maximum benefit for all the children involved, e.g., by placing girls and boys together in work groups and by ensuring that less verbal children are given the opportunity to express themselves during the report.

BE AWARE

Any activity requiring hammer and nails needs careful supervision. Also, it is a good idea to have extra containers on hand in case someone's is unsatisfactory or breaks. Try to choose containers that will last through both water and sand phases of the activity. Firm but pliable plastic containers work better than lightweight, rigid ones, which have a tendency to split. If the children choose to work with foil containers, the holes they punch may result in sharp edges on the inside of the sieve. These easily can be flattened and smoothed out by pressing them down with the head of a nail.

EXTENSIONS

Use the sieves in a sandbox or at a sand table, if one is available. Be sure to alternate regular water play with other structured water experiments. Don't forget to use the scientific method for all structured activities and be sure to include some form of documentation for each. Such experiments might include:

- Pouring water from larger to smaller containers, measuring how many small ones it takes to fill various larger ones, graded according to size.
- Use only suctioning items in water (straws, basters, siphons).

ACTIVITY II

COMPARING HOW SAND AND WATER FLOW THROUGH SIEVES

PURPOSES

- To extend the concept of flow to dry as well as wet media.
- To help children understand the concept of comparison.
- To reinforce the scientific method of inquiry.

WHAT CHILDREN LEARN

- Some of the different properties of wet and dry media.
- How to make comparative observations.
- Listening skills.
- Recording skills.
- Small motor coordination.

FORMAT

A. Large group discussion (10 minutes).
B. Small group activity (15-20 minutes).

MATERIALS AND SUPPLIES

Sieves (from Activity I)

Water table
or large basin around which three or four children can easily work

Sand table
or large basin around which three or four children can easily work

Experience chart paper and marker

Smocks

Paper towels

BACKGROUND INFORMATION

See Activity I for information on water flow. For sand to flow through the sieves it may be necessary to start the action by making a sifting motion, shaking the sieve gently from side to side.

The sound of the sand will vary according to the container from which the sieve is made and how high or low it is held over the basin. For example, a milk carton will make a softer sound than a plastic deli-container, and a foil pan will make a louder sound than both. The higher the sieves are held, the louder the sound. As the sand begins to seep through the holes in the sieve, it makes a pattern revealing each hole. This is caused by the forces of suction and gravity pulling the sand through the holes. The process is especially visible with foil pans, so you may want to plan for every child to have the opportunity to work with a foil sieve.

If the sieve is large enough, it is possible for children to observe the shape the sand flowing through it has made in the basin, e.g., a hill. Water immediately disperses, whereas sand remains where it falls until an external force, such as the wind or a child's hand, causes it to move.

As might be expected, water will flow through a sieve more easily than sand, and both water and sand will flow most easily through the larger and smoother holes where there is less friction to hold it back.

ACTIVITY

A. *Large group discussion*

In a class meeting tell children they are going to work like scientists again. Remind them of the experiment they did with the sieves and water and ask them to tell you what they remember about the experience. Try to elicit details from the children, e.g., that some children used hammers and nails and others just punched holes with the nail, that the water made ripples and bubbles and splashes when it flowed through the sieve into the basin, etc. After they have finished recalling, order the information in sequence — "first we talked about sieves, then each person chose a container and made her or his sieve. We used hammers and nails to make the sieves. We experimented with sieves in colored water," and so on.

Tell the children that now they are going to use their sieves to experiment in sand and water to see how the sieves work with each. Tell them that scientists often experiment in this way to find out how things are alike and different and that this is called comparing. Choose the first group of girls and boys and explain that everyone will have a turn to be a scientist and experiment with sieves in sand and water to compare how they are alike and different.

B. Small group activity

1. Before the children begin to experiment, have them put on smocks.

2. Ask them to think about how sand and water are different and jot down their responses. Ask some questions to spark their thinking:

- How does sand feel (dry, grainy, soft, cool)?
- How does water feel (wet, smooth, cool)?
- Do you think sand can flow through a sieve? Why?
- Do you think sand or water will come out faster? Why?

3. It is important to use the sieves in the sand first, since a wet sieve could introduce variables such as clogging into the experiment and that could confuse the comparisons the children will be making.

4. Let the children work with the sand for several minutes while you record their observations. Again, ask questions to maximize the learning:

- *What will happen if* you shake the sieve gently from side to side?
- Is the sand flowing out of the sieve?
- How does the sand sound when you hold it low over the basin?
- Which sieve makes the loudest sound? the softest sound? Let's listen to each person's sieve and compare the sounds.

- Can you see the sand that has flowed through your sieve into the basin? How does it look?
- Can you see the way the sand flows out of a big hole and a small hole?

5. Be sure to write down the children's observations about the sieves in the sand.

6. After a while ask a transitional question such as "Do you think the water will flow slower or faster than the sand?" Then ask everyone to move over to the water table or basin. Be sure all sand is removed from the sieves, before using them at the water table.

7. As with the sand, let children use their sieves in the water while you take notes on their spontaneous observations. then, ask some questions to clarify their comparisons:

- Did you have to shake the sieve to make the water flow?
- Can you see the water that came out of your sieve in the basin?
- How does the water sound when you hold the sieve high?
- Did the sand make ripples, splashes, bubbles?

8. When the children have finished experimenting with the sieves in water, have them dry their hands and their sieves with paper towels.

9. Have a discussion about the comparisons they found and document them on an experience chart. Be sure to record the experiment according to the scientific method noting their questions, predictions, observations, and conclusions.

10. Repeat the activity in small groups until every child has had a turn.

11. Mount all the experience charts on the wall and have a class discussion comparing how water and sand flow through a sieve.

EQUITY ISSUES

In this activity the group process is most important. Children learn from observing each other's work with the sieves as well as from their own questions and experiences. Validating each child's observations, ensuring that less verbal children contribute to the discussions, and balancing the small groups in terms of girl/boy and dominant/less dominant children all contribute subtly toward the achievement of equity.

BE AWARE

If the sieves go into the water before the sand, they are apt to remain damp no matter how well one tries to dry them. This will most likely lead to clogging of the sand and frustration for the children. It also will add a variable of wet sand to the experiment that will make the wet/dry comparisons difficult to observe. After the experiment is over, however, you may want to let the children try going from water to sand to see what happens (see Extensions). Also if you are using some dry ingredients other than sand with the sieves (see Extensions), do not use salt. A very small amount of salt can be highly toxic if ingested by young children.

EXTENSIONS

After you have completed comparing the flow of sand and water through the sieves, ask the children *"What will happen if* we put the sieve first in the water and then in the sand?" Let the children try it and observe how sand and water when mixed together combine to form a nonflowing substance. Talk about how mixing some things together can change them.

   See how other dry substances flow through a sieve, e.g., sugar, flour, cornstarch. Mix some dry ingredients and water together to see how they change, e.g., sugar and water will produce something quite different from cornstarch and water. Discuss and record the children's observations.

BLOCKS

Exploring Momentum with Ramps and Balls

OVERVIEW

Blocks are an essential component of the early childhood curriculum, and there has been much written about the potential contribution of blocks for early childhood learning. In *The Block Book*, a popular NAEYC publication, the authors discuss the many ways blocks can provide a material for learning through play: in art, social studies, self-expression, dramatic play, science, and math. Through block play, young children learn about the properties of matter and about stability and balance. Visual-spatial skills are developed by building towers and bridging structures, and foundations are laid for understanding geometric concepts of length, width, area, volume, and number.

The activities that follow affirm and extend the kind of mathematic and scientific learning that is afforded through block play. Through simple experiments in a format familiar to young children — building ramps and rolling down balls — principles of physics are explored. In these experiments, children predict, conduct, observe, conclude, and document their findings. By incorporating the scientific method into structured experiments, the activities extend block play in new ways.

Teachers found remarkable children's enthusiasm for participating in this kind of activity and the learning it fosters. Children worked in groups of three while they conducted the experiment in the hallway outside their classroom. It didn't take long for the word to spread that something exciting was happening. The activity took place over several days, and children began observing from the doorway. As later groups participated, it became clear that other children had already told them what the experiment was about. The children also kept track, on their own, of who had participated and who still had not had the opportunity.

The activities are structured in such a way that girls and boys participate as equals. For, while educators acknowledge that the kind of learning in block building is essential for all children, both research and anecdotal information tell us that boys continue to gravitate toward the block area and girls often do not.

The Blocks activities include:

Activity I   *The Effect of Inclined Planes on Speed and Distance*
Activity II   *Analyzing the Results*
Activity III   *The Effect of Weight on Speed and Distance*

ACTIVITY I

THE EFFECT OF INCLINED PLANES ON SPEED AND DISTANCE

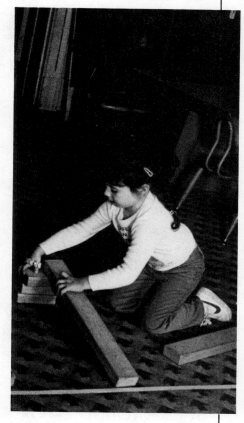

PURPOSES

- To help children develop the processes of experimentation: predicting, conducting, observing, concluding, and documenting.
- To explore the effect of different angles of inclined planes on speed and distance.

WHAT CHILDREN LEARN

- How to set up a scientific experiment.
- How to record an experiment.
- The effect of the height of a ramp on the speed and distance of an object.
- Math skills, e.g., measuring distance.
- Visual-spatial skills.

FORMAT

A. Large group discussion (10 minutes).

B. Small group activity (15-20 minutes per group).

MATERIALS AND SUPPLIES

Six unit blocks (5½" long)

Six quadruple unit blocks (22" long)

One small hard ball
e.g., a handball or racquet ball

Masking tape

Easel paper and magic marker

Stick-on dots
in four different colors, e.g.,

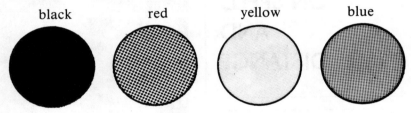

black   red   yellow   blue

BACKGROUND INFORMATION

During this experiment, children will set up three block ramps so that they form angles of three different heights, and then they will roll a ball down each of the ramps. What they will observe is the relationship between speed and distance. The higher the angle of the ramp, the faster and farther the ball will roll. As the angle of the ramp gets closer to the ground, the speed and distance of the ball keeps decreasing. For example, if a quadruple block was placed directly on the ground, a ball placed on it would hardly move at all.

For this experiment to work properly, it needs to be set up in an area that is long enough to allow room for the ball that rolls down the highest ramp to come to a stop on its own. For example, one teacher used a hallway outside the classroom. The experiment also could be set up in a gym or outdoors. It is important that there be no obstacles, e.g., a table leg or an area rug, in the path of the balls. Also, a slant in the floor or the pile of a rug might affect the direction of a ball or impede its roll. To ensure that the experiment will work and to avoid frustration on the children's part, it would be best to set it up and try it out yourself before beginning with the children.

Also, as is discussed in "Using The Scientific Method with Young Children: How To Do It," for the experiment to be reliable, it needs to be set up in exactly the same manner each time it is conducted.

ACTIVITY

A. *Large group discussion*

At circle time, or a class meeting, explain to children that during the next few days they all will be participating in a science experiment. Talk about the various aspects of an experiment: children will predict, conduct, conclude, and document. If you have made a collage (see "Preliminary Activity"), refer back to it and talk about what scientists do.

B. *Small group activity*

1. Prepare documentation charts on easel paper beforehand (see sample at end of activity).

2. With groups of three children at a time, go to a designated area and tell children that they are going to be scientists and do an experiment. Explain that each person is going to build a ramp with blocks and then see how far a ball will roll down it.

3. Ask the children to help you place a strip of masking tape along the floor so that the bottoms of the ramps will line up and the ball will always start from the same place.

4. Give each child two quadruple unit blocks plus either one, two, or three unit blocks.

5. Ask the child with the one unit block to build a ramp so that the bottom of the ramp ends at the strip of masking tape. The ramp should be the width of the two quadruple blocks, placed on top of the unit block that has been laid down on the floor.

6. Ask the other children to build a ramp two unit blocks high and three unit blocks high. All the ramps should line up along the masking tape. Point out to the children that, since this is a science experiment, it is important that all their ramps be built in the same manner.

7. Once the ramps are built, take the ball and ask the children, *"What will happen if* you roll this ball down your ramp?" Ask, "How far do you think the ball will roll?"

8. Have each child predict where she or he thinks the ball will stop rolling and go stand where that predicted spot is. Have each child mark her or his prediction spot with a black stick-on dot.

9. After children have marked their predictions, ask each child to conduct the experiment by rolling the ball down her or his ramp.

Point out that, for this experiment, they can't push or throw the ball down the ramp. They should place the ball on the top of their ramps and just let go. If children give the ball an extra "push," ask them to do it again and gently remind them that they are conducting a scientific experiment.

10. Children might need to experiment with their ramp a few times. It is also a good idea to have children go sit or stand where their ball comes to a stop to experience the distance with their bodies.

11. When they are finished, ask them what happened. What did each child observe? Some questions you might ask include:

• Did the ball go farther than you predicted?

• Did the ball not go as far as you predicted?

• Whose ball actually rolled the farthest?

• Whose ball stopped closest to the ramp?

12. After children have finished discussing their observations, have them draw some conclusions. You might ask:

• Why do you think one ball rolled farther than another?

• Did any of the balls roll faster than the others?

• Why did it go farther?

Eventually, help children understand that the higher the ramp, the faster and farther the ball will roll. During the pilot testing, children on their own began to test out their newly-discovered theory. They took turns rolling the ball down each other's ramps. They wanted to make sure that it didn't matter who rolled the ball down the ramp, that indeed it was the angle of the ramp that made the difference.

13. Once children have finished discussing their observations and conclusions, give each child two stick-on dots of the same color, i.e., one should have two blue dots, one two red dots, and one two yellow dots. Then have each child use one dot to mark her or his ramp and the other to mark where her or his ball actually stopped rolling. Be sure that the designations are constant, i.e., that all yellow dots represent three-block ramps, all red dots the two-block ramps, all blue dots the one-block ramp.

14. Explain to children that, as scientists, they are now going to document their observations — they are going to make a chart so other people can see what they have learned. The kind of chart they are making is called a "data dot" chart.

15. On the chart you have prepared, have children identify their ramp and mark it with an appropriate color stick-on dot. Then

have them take another stick-on dot and approximate on the chart how far the ball rolled. It is not necessary that the charts be measured exactly, just that they reflect that the higher the ramp, the farther the ball rolled. (See end of activity for one of the charts made by the children.) If possible, hang up the data dot charts, so as each group finishes its experiment, its chart will add to a growing science atmosphere in the classroom and school.

EQUITY ISSUES

Both formal research and anecdotal information from classroom teachers attest to the fact that boys gravitate to the block area more frequently than girls. Because this block activity is removed from the regular block area, and because all children are required to participate in the experiment, it allows girls and boys to participate as equals. You may, however, have to ensure that this happens. For example, be sure that children who do not speak up easily are not dominated by those who do. You may want to ask one child to wait and give a classmate a chance to speak first. Groups should be a mix of girls and boys, and all children should be given an equal chance to predict, conduct, observe, conclude, and document.

BE AWARE

Some children may have trouble getting their ball to roll straight down the ramp. If this happens you might suggest that they kneel down directly behind their ramps rather than off to one side.

EXTENSIONS

Documentation of the experiment provides a good opportunity for a measuring activity. During the pilot test, children discerned several different ways of measuring. Some counted the diamond pattern on the floor in the corridor where the experiment was conducted. One girl used her body as a measure, stretching her arm on a diagonal between her prediction dot and the place where the ball actually rolled. For another group of children, the teacher provided unit blocks, which the children lined up and counted as a form of measurement.

OUR SCIENCE EXPERIMENT

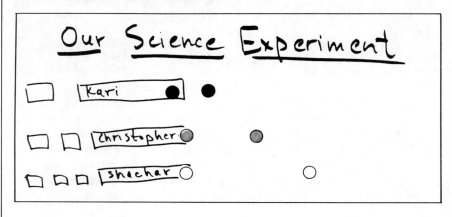

ACTIVITY II

ANALYZING THE RESULTS

PURPOSES

- To help children understand how to interpret information from charts and generalize the results.
- To help children extrapolate data, i.e., predict answers to new and related questions based on previous results.

WHAT CHILDREN LEARN

- Analytical skills.
- Interpretation of data.
- Generalization of data.
- How to predict answers based on previous results.

FORMAT

A. Large group discussion (15 minutes).

B. Small group activity (ongoing).

MATERIALS AND SUPPLIES

Data dot charts from Block Activity I

BACKGROUND INFORMATION

By looking at the charts and seeing that the results of all experiments are the same, it is possible to generalize that this always will be the case. It is also possible, based on these previous results, to predict the answers to new and related questions.

ACTIVITY

A. Large group discussion

Hang up all the charts in one area of the classroom. During circle or meeting time, ask children to look at all the charts and ask them what the charts tell them about the experiment. Once children realize that the ball that rolled down the highest ramp always rolled the farthest, ask them, *"What will happen if we do the experiment again?"* Ask them "How can we change the experiment a little?" Some additional questions you might ask include:

- *What will happen if* you roll a ball down a ramp that is four blocks high?
- *What will happen if* you place the ball on a block that is flat on the ground?

B. Small group activity

Children should continue to work in their groups to test out their new predictions. Children might decide to build ramps four and five blocks high and roll the ball down to see how far it rolls. Or they might decide to place a block on the ground and see what happens to the ball.

EQUITY ISSUES

Studies have shown that during the elementary grades girls are nervous about making generalizations and extrapolating from previous results. They don't trust what they have found. Their lack of confidence leads them to avoid "making a guess," which they perceive as taking a risk. Boys, on the other hand, tend to extrapolate with too little data. Both need help in redressing these deficits from an early age. Girls, especially, need to be encouraged to experiment with new things.

BE AWARE

It is important to remember that extrapolation can be extended only so far. The closer the question is to what you already know, the more the prediction is apt to be accurate. For example, you can ask children what will happen if the ramps are four or five blocks high. But if the ramp gets much higher, the angle will "disappear" and a vertical drop will occur.

EXTENSIONS

Children should be encouraged to retest their predictions from time to time. They also should be encouraged to think of their own variations, e.g., *what will happen if* we use different rolling items such as a car, a small wheelchair, or other wheeled objects?

ACTIVITY III

THE EFFECT OF WEIGHT ON SPEED AND DISTANCE

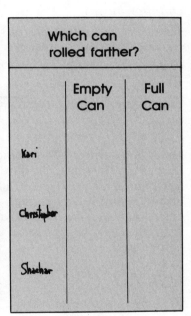

Which can rolled farther?		
	Empty Can	Full Can
Kari		
Christopher		
Shachar		

Tally Sheet

PURPOSES

- To set up a simple outdoor experiment.
- To develop further children's skills of predicting, conducting, observing, concluding, and documenting.
- To explore the effect of weight on speed and distance.

WHAT CHILDREN LEARN

- The effect of the weight of an object on how fast and far it will roll.
- How to set up a scientific experiment.

- How to record an experiment.
- Visual-spatial skills.
- Large muscle coordination.

FORMAT

A. Large group discussion (10 minutes).

B. Small group outdoor activity (15-20 minutes).

C. Large group follow-up discussion (10 minutes).

MATERIALS AND SUPPLIES

Outdoor blocks

Two cans with identical tops and bottoms
e.g., coffee or nut cans, one emptied and one full

Experience chart paper and markers

BACKGROUND INFORMATION

During this experiment, children will roll different weight objects down a ramp. What will happen is that the heavier object will roll faster and farther. The momentum increases because of the mass — the heavier the mass, the harder it is to stop the object and the farther it will go. This experiment, like Activity I, needs an area that has no obstacles and is long enough for the heavier object to come to a stop on its own. An outdoor area or large gym space is suggested. Once again, it would be best to set up the experiment and try it out yourself beforehand.

ACTIVITY

A. Large group discussion

Before you go outdoors, explain to children that when they go outside, they are going to have a chance to work like scientists and conduct another experiment with ramps. Let children examine the one full and one empty can. Ask them to describe how they are the same and how they are different. Ask children to predict *what will happen if* they roll these two cans down the same ramp? Write children's predictions on a large sheet of paper.

B. Small group activity

1. Prepare tally sheet beforehand (see sample at end of activity).

2. Once outdoors, ask one group of children to begin to set up the experiment. (It might be a good idea to continue to have

children work in the same small groups as in Activity I.) Have the group build a ramp of any height. Have each child hold the cans and predict where she or he thinks each one will roll. Then ask each child to roll each can down the ramp (can should not be pushed or thrown) and observe what happens.

3. Have each group document its observations on the tally sheet and bring the sheet back to classroom for a group discussion (depending on size of class and time outdoors, this activity may have to extend over a period of days).

C. Large group follow-up discussion

After all children have had the opportunity to participate in the experiment, hang up the tally sheet in the class and discuss what was observed. To help children understand that the reason one can went farther, you might talk about concepts of heavy and light, near and far, fast and slow.

Look at children's original hypotheses to see if what they predicted would happen turned out to be true. Add children's new hypotheses, if any.

Ask children to think about what happened during their first experiment with ramps and balls. Ask them why did the object roll farther during that experiment, e.g., height of ramps? Why did the object roll farther this time, e.g., weight of object?

EQUITY ISSUES

As with block play, boys traditionally have more experience with building and large motor play in general. Having girls and boys work together building a large ramp is a positive equity experience.

BE AWARE

The cans you use in this experiment must be identical — the only variable is to be the weight of the can. The top and bottom of the can need to be exactly the same. Any variation, e.g., a juice or soda can with a heavier plastic flip-top lid, will cause the can to roll at an angle. Coffee or nut cans, where the whole top can be removed with a can opener, should work well. It is always wise to try them out first. Be sure there are no sharp edges when you remove the top of the can.

EXTENSIONS

If outdoor blocks are not available, the experiment can be done using a slide. Children might also experiment with pushing the empty and full cans to find out how much more human energy is required to push the full can up the ramp or slide.

BOTTLES AND LIQUIDS

Exploring Solubility, Density, and Viscosity

OVERVIEW

When two liquids are put together in the same bottle, different things can happen. If the liquids are soluble, they will mix and become one new liquid. If they are not, they will stay in separate layers. Shaking the bottle, or turning it upside down will cause other things to happen. This kind of activity is fun, but it is also the basis for some complex learning. By working with different liquids and seeing how they interact, and by dropping objects through different liquids and observing the rates at which they fall, children begin to explore such concepts as solubility, density, and viscosity. They also learn about gravity and the effects of different liquids on gravity's pull.

In the following activities, children use their five senses to determine differences among liquids. With these activities, as in many other early childhood activities, children use and trust their senses as tools. Children's senses become a part of the "scientific method" as they see, hear, touch, smell, and taste to collect "data" and to formulate and answer questions. An experience chart is suggested as the means to document the children's experiences in all three activities. This is because words, rather than graphs or charts, can best describe the sensory, visual, and aesthetic nature of these activities.

Teachers have found the activities easy to do and helpful to the children in areas such as prediction, reasoning, and working cooperatively. Children, working with bottles and liquids, have been enthusiastic and involved. In the words of their teachers, children "stretch their minds a little."

Both children and teachers discovered another dimension to "Bottles and Liquids" — one of aesthetics. They learned that the combinations and colors of different liquids can be beautiful as can the different shapes created as the liquids flow through each other. And as the following poem, created by a kindergartner shows, relationship between science and beauty was found.

About Bottles

The white is like the white stuff in the sky.
The shiny things are like rainbows
And are like rain falling down
The blue is like the sky.

By Kenroy

The Bottles and Liquids activities include:

Activity I   *Using Our Senses to Explore Liquids*

Activity II   *Two in One*

Activity II   *Traveling Through Different Liquids*

ACTIVITY I

USING OUR SENSES TO EXPLORE LIQUIDS

PURPOSES

- To provide a sensory approach to scientific inquiry.
- To help children understand the properties of different liquids.

WHAT CHILDREN LEARN

- Observation skills.
- New vocabulary.
- That their senses help them to learn.

FORMAT

Small group activity and discussion (15 minutes).

MATERIALS AND SUPPLIES

Small bowls
three for every six children

Light Karo (corn) syrup

Vegetable oil

Water

Paper towels

Experience chart paper and marker

BACKGROUND INFORMATION

The liquids for all the "Bottles and Liquids" activities are the same — vegetable oil, light Karo (corn) syrup, and water. The major differences of these liquids are:

Density — oil is the lightest (least dense); syrup is the heaviest (most dense).

Smell — syrup has the strongest odor; usually water has the most neutral odor. (If your water has a number of minerals, this may not be the case.)

Color — while the oil is yellower than the other two, the light syrup and water are approximately the same color.

Viscosity (the degree of friction or stickiness of the liquids) — the syrup is the stickiest, while the oil is the most lubricating.

ACTIVITY

A. Small group activity

1. Form groups of six children with an adult for each group. If an adult is not available for each group, you may want to do the activity over several days.

2. Explain to the children that they will be using their senses to explore different liquids. Review each of the five senses and what they do.

3. For each group, pour an equal amount of water, oil, and Karo (corn) syrup in three identical bowls.

4. Have the children use all of their senses to find differences in the liquids. Ask them to look at the three liquids and see how they look different. then ask the children to smell each of the liquids. When they have finished looking and smelling, ask each

child to put one finger in the syrup, feel it, and then taste it. After wiping their fingers on a damp paper towel, ask children to touch and taste the oil, wipe, and then touch and taste the water. Finally, the adult can shake each of the bowls gently while children listen to hear if there are any differences in the sounds of the liquids.

B. *Small group discussion*

After each group has finished exploring with their five senses, have a discussion about the differences they found. Ask children to discuss the differences by sight, by smell, by touch, by taste, and by sound. Make an experience chart with the children to document the activity. Encourage descriptive vocabulary to describe the sensory nature of the activity. Some of the observations children have made about the liquids are "The syrup looks like Jell-o." "The syrup is stickier than the others." "The oil is yellower."

EQUITY ISSUES

At first some children may not be comfortable touching unfamiliar substances. This is part of the "yucky" attitude that begins early and continues to impede many children's (most often girls) pursuance of science throughout school. For example, there may be a reluctance to handle snails or snakes, to dissect laboratory animals, or to handle internal organs. Therefore, it is important that all children have the opportunity to try this experiment and that you provide special support and encouragement to those children who show reluctance.

BE AWARE

While differences between liquids such as oil and syrup might be quite apparent to an adult, children may not be able to easily distinguish between them. Be sure to allow ample time for children to explore each liquid and clarify any confusion that may occur.

EXTENSIONS

While this activity focuses on using the senses to find differences, other sources of differences can be explored such as weight or rate at which the liquids pour. In addition, other liquids can be used to do the activity e.g., other kinds of syrup, different juices, vinegar, or molasses.

Priscilla Caine, kindergarten teacher at School Number Four, Lawrence Public Schools, suggested the foregoing activity.

ACTIVITY II

TWO
IN
ONE

PURPOSES

- To help children begin to explore ways liquids interact.
- To help children begin to understand the concept of insolubility.
- To encourage children to describe what they see.

WHAT CHILDREN LEARN

- Observation skills.
- How liquids of different densities interact.
- New vocabulary.
- The aesthetics of science.

FORMAT

A. Large group discussion (10 minutes).
B. Small group activity (15-20 minutes for each small group).
C. Large group discussion (15 minutes).

MATERIALS AND SUPPLIES

Clear plastic bottle with cap
with the label soaked off, e.g., 18 oz. shampoo bottle

Vegetable oil

Water

Food coloring

Experience chart paper and markers

BACKGROUND INFORMATION

If two liquids will not combine when they are mixed, then the liquids are insoluble, i.e., one liquid will not dissolve in the other. Oil and water are two common insoluble liquids. Soluble liquids are those, such as water and milk, that will combine when mixed to form one liquid.

If two insoluble liquids are combined in a bottle, no matter how much they are shaken, the heavier (or denser) liquid will settle to the bottom and the lighter liquid will rise to the top. In this activity, oil is lighter (or less dense) than water.

When you shake a bottle with two insoluble liquids in it, three different types of bubbles form. These are 1) air bubbles rising to the top of the bottle, 2) bubbles of the lighter liquid also rising and 3) bubbles of the heavier liquid falling to the bottom of the bottle.

ACTIVITY

A. Large group discussion

1. Prepare the bottle beforehand.

a) Empty a clear shampoo bottle, soak off the label, and clean thoroughly.
b) Fill the bottle with one cup of food-colored water. Use any color but yellow, which is too close to the color of oil.
c) Add one cup of oil to the bottle.
d) Screw the cap back on tightly.

2. During circle time talk about what children learned about oil and water when they used their senses in Activity I. Ask them what they think will happen when two of the liquids they used in the earlier activity are put in one bottle.

B. Small group activity

1. Work with groups of four children with the bottle. Give children ample time to explore freely and formulate their own

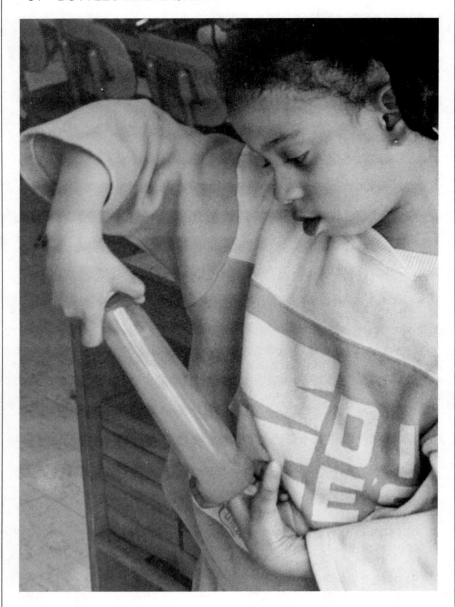

questions. Later, you might want to pose some additional questions:

- *What will happen if* we shake the bottle?
- *What will happen if* we turn the bottle upside down?
- Which liquid goes to the bottom? Is it always the same? Why?

2. Write down the children's questions and observations. Make sure each child has an opportunity to work with the bottle. This may take several days.

C. *Large group discussion*

1. When all the children have worked with the bottle, have them come together in a large group. Show them the bottle and ask what they observed. Help the children draw some conclusions about the liquids in the bottle. Children have drawn conclusions such as "The water goes to the bottom." "There are different kinds of bubbles." "When you shake the bottle, it makes a different color."

2. With the children, make an experience chart to document the experiment. You may want to introduce the word insoluble, i.e., "doesn't mix." Be sure the chart includes which liquid always fell to the bottom and why. Mount the chart in the room. Put the bottle on a table where children can continue to work with it individually or in small groups.

EQUITY ISSUES

Be sure each child has a chance to work with the bottle, draw conclusions, and to share those conclusions with others. Be sure that the groups consist of both girls and boys whenever possible.

BE AWARE

Do not use plastic bottles with spouts or pour caps. It is very difficult to make those caps leakproof.

EXTENSIONS

Prepare the bottle a second time and change the color of the water. For example, if you color the water red, when you shake the bottle, varying shades of orange will appear. If the water is blue, when shaken, varying shades of blueish green will appear. Yellow food coloring is not recommended, however, since the contrast with the oil is not sharp enough.

Explore soluble liquids as well as insoluble ones. After the children have finished experimenting with oil and water, pour milk into a bottle and then pour in some water. Shake up the bottle and have the children watch the milk and water combine. Discuss the differences between what happened when the milk and water were shaken in a bottle and what happened when the oil and water were shaken in a bottle.

ACTIVITY III

TRAVELING THROUGH DIFFERENT LIQUIDS

PURPOSES

- To help children explore how the same object acts in different mediums.
- To help children begin to explore the concept of gravity.

WHAT CHILDREN LEARN

- Observation skills.
- Information about viscosity and its effect on an object as it falls through different liquids.
- Independent work skills.
- Vocabulary skills.
- Recording skills.

FORMAT

A. Large group discussion (10 minutes).
B. Small group activity (15-30 minutes).
C. Large group discussion (15 minutes).

MATERIALS AND SUPPLIES

Two identical clear plastic bottles and caps
e.g., 18 oz. shampoo bottles with the labels soaked off

Two identical small screws

Light Karo (corn) syrup

Water

Experience chart paper and marker

BACKGROUND INFORMATION

When the objects are placed in the bottles, or when the bottles are turned upside down, the objects will fall to the bottom of the bottle. Gravity, the pull of the earth on objects close to it, causes the objects in the bottles to "fall."

The speed of a falling object is influenced by the medium (liquid or gas) through which it is falling. For example, an object will fall faster in air than in glue. The stickier, or more viscous, the liquid in which an object is falling, the slower the object will fall. Since syrup is the most viscous liquid in this activity, the object will fall slower in it. Since water has very little viscosity, the object will fall quickly.

ACTIVITY

A. Large group discussion

1. Prepare the bottles beforehand.

a) Empty the shampoo bottles, soak off the labels, and clean thoroughly.
b) Fill one bottle with two cups of water, put one screw in it, and put the cap back on tightly.
c) Fill the second bottle with two cups of light Karo (corn) syrup, place the screw in it, and put the cap on tightly.

2. During circle time, talk about what children learned about syrup and water when they used their senses in Activity I. Be sure they remember that the syrup looked and felt much stickier than the water.

3. Explain to the children that they are now going to observe what happens when objects go through different liquids.

B. Small group activity

Work with groups of four children with the bottles. Allow ample time for each child to explore the bottles. Ask *what will happen if* the bottles are turned upside down. Help children observe the speed of the screw, the sound it makes in each liquid, the difference in bubbles, the way the liquid runs down the sides of the bottles. Keep notes on their observations.

It is a good idea to have small bowls of water and Karo (corn) syrup on the table with the bottles so children can make the connection between how the liquids feel and how the objects fall through them in the bottles. Over a period of several days, have all of the children work with the bottles.

C. Large group discussion

When all the children have worked with the bottles, have them come together in a large group. With the children make an experience chart to document the experiment. Be sure it includes in which liquid the screw fell more slowly and in which one the screw fell more quickly, and why. Children might enjoy using the words viscous and viscosity. Mount this bottle experience chart next to the ones from the previous activities. Set the bottles out on a table near the charts so children can continue to explore them on their own.

EQUITY ISSUES

Early physics experiences such as the bottle activities are important for all children. Since traditionally girls do not choose to take physics courses in high school and beyond, it is essential that they begin to have these experiences very early.

BE AWARE

If the small object you put in the bottles doesn't sink, much of the purpose of the activity is lost. Before doing the activity with the children, check to make sure the screws you selected will sink, not float. Also, most screws (except for galvanized ones) rust in water after a few weeks, so you will want to replace the screw with an identical one and change the water frequently. It would be interesting to let the children problem-solve about why the screw rusts in water but not in syrup (the more viscous material coats and lubricates the screw).

EXTENSIONS

Take the two bottles from this activity and, in addition to the screws, add lighter objects, e.g., paper clips, small safety pins, sequins. Have children observe the different rates at which different objects fall. Some objects might float in the syrup, but fall in the water. There will be no observable difference between a paper clip and a screw falling through the water, but a paper clip will fall visibly slower than a screw in the syrup.

Our Science Story

We worked like scientists. We had two bottles. One had water and a screw in it. The other bottle had syrup and a screw in it. Sara said "The syrup was very sticky." Everyone had a chance to turn the bottle upside down. Here is what we saw.

Toni: the screw falls very, very fast in the water.
José: You could hear it drop
Sarita: It went ZOOM!
Timmy: In the syrup the screw fell very, very slow.
Terry: That's because the syrup is so thick.
Lisa: It sort of floated down.
Jake: I like to watch the syrup drip down the sides of the bottle. I liked to watch that.

Ms. Lopez said we were good scientists. We observed the bottles and thought about what was happening.

She taught us another word for sticky. It is viscous.

MACHINES AND ME

Technology in the Early Childhood Classroom

OVERVIEW

American life depends on machines. Machines are everywhere, from the stick a person might use as a lever to help move a rock to the sophisticated computers that guide the space shuttle. Yet in spite of the pervasiveness of machines, they often are taken for granted, and few of us know much about how they work. Many times it seems "magic" that a car runs or that a computer works. Because of inexperience with machines, teachers, for the most part, don't provide opportunities for children to explore machines and how they work.

There are many good reasons to include machines in the early childhood classroom. Many children, both boys and girls, are fascinated by machines. Learning how they work helps to develop visual-spatial and problem-solving skills. In addition, since children are living in an age of technology, it is important for them to understand people's roles in developing and controlling its use.

While some children have the opportunity to explore machines outside of school, many do not. And girls are among the "many who do not." In our society, machines and tinkering are seen as appropriate activities for boys but not girls. Outside of school most boys are expected to take apart a clock or play with an engine, while few girls are encouraged in this direction and most are discouraged. If machines are made part of the curriculum, many girls will have a chance to develop a degree of comfort with machines and technology.

"Machines and Me" has been designed to make learning about and using machines an interesting and fun part of an early childhood curriculum for girls, boys, and for their teachers. As part of each activity, background information is provided about how the machines work. The activities focus on machines that are both easy to find and safe, machines that children and teachers see and use every day.

The initital activities introduce children to machines and help them identify machines in the class, in their homes, and in the world. In later activities, technology is demystified by having teachers and children tinker — take machines apart to see how they work and what can be learned from them.

Teachers have found the activities easy to use and to incorporate into the classroom, while children were both interested and involved. For example, during the pilot testing, two girls found reassembling a food grinder a real challenge. In spite of their initial problems figuring out how to put the grinder together, they would not let anyone, adult or child, help them. After a while they figured out what to do. As they finished, they both yelled, "We did it by ourselves," and the class applauded.

The Machines and Me activities include:

Activity I   *Machines in School and at Home*
Activity II   *Machine Books and Collages*
Activity III *Classroom Technology*
Activity IV *Setting Up a Technology Center*
Activity V   *Taking Technology Trips*

ACTIVITY I

MACHINES IN SCHOOL AND AT HOME

Machines in Room 28

1. juice can opener
2. stapler (3)
3. telephone (3)
4. pulley (small)
5. scissors
6. weighing machine
7. pulley (large)
8. funnel
9. hole puncher
10. can opener
11. clock
12. film strip projector

PURPOSES

- To help children learn what machines are.
- To increase children's awareness of how machines extend human ability.
- To increase the interest of all children in machines.

WHAT CHILDREN LEARN

- What machines are.
- The names and functions of familiar machines.
- Math skills, e.g., to categorize and make sets of machines.
- Beginning research skills.

FORMAT

A. Large group discussion and classroom tour (15 minutes).

B. Large group discussion (10 minutes).

MATERIALS AND SUPPLIES

Large construction paper and markers

BACKGROUND INFORMATION

A machine is something that is constructed or built to transmit motion, energy, or force. Machines make tasks easier for people to do. One of the most basic machines is the lever and fulcrum (a seesaw is an example of a lever and fulcrum). Using a lever and fulcrum to lift a weight is a lot less work than just lifting it. In fact, there is an old saying that one could move the world if one could just find a lever long enough and a place to stand.

In the classroom or in the world, people are surrounded by machines. Many machines however, are not recognized as such. In the classroom some of the machines that can be found are: light switches, lights, pencil sharpeners, door hinges and doorknobs, telephones, tape dispensers, wheels and axles on pull toys, bikes, wheelchairs, the food cart, water faucets, and toilet flushing mechanisms. Desks and chairs are not machines because they don't do anything. Doorknobs are machines because they transmit the motion of turning the knob into moving the latch so the door can be opened.

ACTIVITIES

A. *Large group discussion and classroom tour*

In a large group, talk about machines with the children. Ask them "what is a machine?" Discuss with them how machines help us work and make our jobs easier. Have the children name some machines and talk about how they work. Examples can be as simple as the wheels that make it easier to pull things around or as complex as the school buses that make it easier to come to school.

Have the children look around the classroom and find all the machines they can. As each child mentions a machine, ask the group what the machine does. With the children, make a list of "Machines in Our Classroom." Some children may want to draw pictures of the machines. Hang up the list in the classroom.

B. *Large group discussion*

Talk with the children about some of the machines they have at home, such as egg beaters, TV sets, or refrigerators. Suggest that the children go home and look for machines.

At circle time the next day, talk about the machines children found at home and what they do. Make a list of "Machines in Our Homes." Hang it next to the "Machines in Our Classroom" list.

BE AWARE

The children will come up with some "machines" that may or may not be machines. A rule of thumb is, if it is active, it is a machine, if it is passive, it is not.

EQUITY ISSUES

It is important that children understand that everyone regardless of sex, race, or disability can and does work with machines. When choosing pictures for the classroom walls, for bulletin boards, and for classroom activities such as collaging be sure to search for illustrations that show a diversity of women and men operating and fixing machines.

If a child in your classroom uses a hearing aid, it would be an opportunity to discuss this machine in the context of technology. A wheelchair (manually or electrically operated) could be discussed in the same context.

EXTENSIONS

After discussing machines the children found at school and at home, have them use their imaginations to think up some machines they would like to invent — such as a machine to pick up their clothes. Children could report on their machines, write stories, and draw pictures. Bind the stories and put them in the classroom library.

ACTIVITY II

MACHINE BOOKS AND COLLAGES

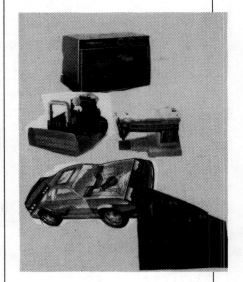

PURPOSES

- To help children understand the role of machines in daily life.
- To increase the visibility of machines in the classroom.

WHAT CHILDREN LEARN

- Increased awareness of different machines.
- Names and functions of different machines.
- Small motor coordination.

FORMAT

A. Large group discussion and collage-making (20-30 minutes).
B. Individual work (ongoing).

MATERIALS AND SUPPLES

Large sheet of paper
for collage

Magazines
such as *National Geographic, Scientific American, Sports and Spokes, Family Computing, Classroom Computer, Learning, Ladies Home Journal,* and others that carry pictures of machines

Scissors

Glue

BACKGROUND INFORMATION

There are a great number of different types of machines. These include machines related to transportation — cars, buses, wheelchairs, airplanes, motor boats, trains, bicycles, roller skates; food processing machines — can openers, stoves, refrigerators, egg beaters, toasters, coffee and spice grinders, coffee makers; business machines — typewriters, computers, pencil sharpeners, air conditioners, elevators, copiers, calculators, postage machines.

ACTIVITIES

A. *Large group discussion and collage-making*

Collect a number of magazines with pictures of a variety of machines. Include science-oriented publications such as *Scientific American,* general interest magazines such as *McCalls,* computer magazines such as *Creative Computing,* and car magazines such as *Road and Track.*

Take down the lists and drawings the children have made previously about machines and have a discussion about the many machines they discovered in the classroom and in their homes. Bring out the magazines and ask children to look for pictures of machines to cut out and make into a collage. Show the children some examples of different types of machines pictured in the magazines. Have them go through the magazines and find pictures of additional machines. Have the children make collages out of the pictures they have cut out.

B. *Individual work (ongoing)*

After the children have completed their collage, have them begin to make individual books about the machines they use. The books can be composed of drawings and/or pictures from magazines. As children learn about and use more machines, have them make drawings or find pictures of the ''new machines'' and put them in the machine books. As children's experiences with machines grow, so will their machine books.

EQUITY ISSUES

Be sure to have pictures that show women and men using machines in nonstereotypical ways for the collage and machine books. For example, have pictures of women fixing cars and men using kitchen appliances.

Remember that the children's machine books will be reflecting their experiences with machines. From time to time check the children's books to see if they reflect that girls and boys are "experiencing" a variety of machines. If not, provide them with additional opportunities and again reinforce the ideas that all machines are for both sexes.

EXTENSIONS

Check the picture books in the classroom to see if any include girls and boys working with machines. Consider including books about children and machines in the class library (see "Resources").

After the children have completed the class collage, you could have children make individual collages using sets of machines, e.g., food machines, machines with wheels, business machines, industrial machines.

ACTIVITY III

CLASSROOM TECHNOLOGY

PURPOSES

- To demonstrate the functioning of some everyday machines.
- To encourage children to take machines apart to see how they work.

WHAT CHILDREN LEARN

- Problem-solving skills.
- Visual-spatial skills.
- To recognize familiar shapes in machine parts.
- The fun of tinkering.
- Small motor coordination.
- Self-esteem.

FORMAT

A. Large group discussion (10 minutes).

B. Individual and small group work (15 minutes).

C. Large group discussion (20 minutes).

MATERIALS AND SUPPLES

Hand food grinder

Food
carrots or shelled nuts

Plates

BACKGROUND INFORMATION

A food grinder was selected because it is an interesting machine and has a small number of relatively large parts that can be put back together by four-, five-, and six-year-olds. In addition, the grinder works both before the children take it apart and after they put it back together. Most importantly, the grinder is safe to take apart and put together and is safe to use. Food grinders last forever and can be used for many years. Parents and grandparents may be willing to donate old food grinders.

Before you do this activity with the class, be sure that you know how to take the grinder apart and put it back together. Food grinders work by turning the handle. As you turn the handle, the spiral core pushes the food against the graters or grinders, which cut it into small pieces. The pressure causes the food to push through the grinder holes and come out on the other side.

ACTIVITY

A. Large group discussion

At circle time, introduce the food grinder to the children by asking if any children have ever seen or used one. Ask one child to demonstrate it by grinding some food. If vegetables are used, wash them first so that the children can eat them after they are ground. Explain to children that they all will have a chance to experiment with the food grinder.

B. Individual and small group work

1. Set up the grinder and have small groups of two to three children grind some shelled nuts or carrots. Be sure that every child experiences the grinding process. Have the children watch

the grinding and figure out how the grinder works. Be sure to save the ground food.

2. Have the children take the food grinder apart (remind them they will be putting it back together) and wash and dry the pieces.

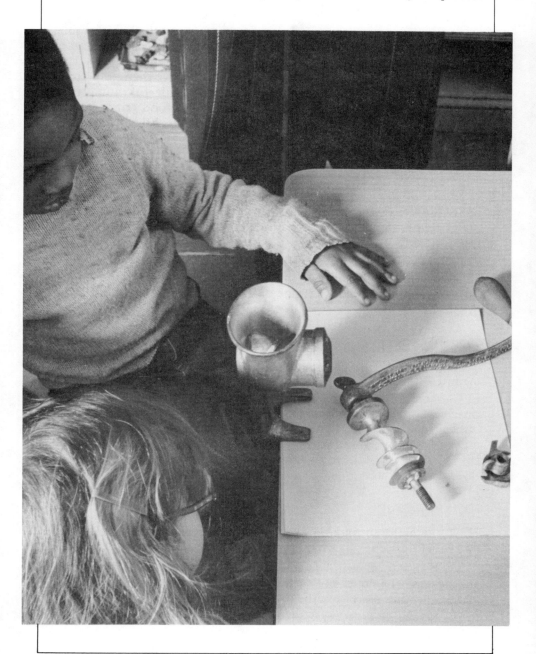

3. Have the children reassemble the food grinder. Remember that some children will take longer than others to do this. Provide support, but encourage the children to put the grinder together by themselves.

C. *Large group discussion*

Take the ground food and use it to make a snack. For example, the carrots can be combined with raisins to make carrot salad or ground peanuts (peanut butter), can be spread on crackers. Talk with the children about what they learned. Have them talk about the different pieces of the grinder — their wonderful round spiral and octagonal shapes — and what makes the food grinder work. Also ask children to describe how they felt about putting the grinder back together.

BE AWARE

It is very difficult to accidently hurt yourself taking a food grinder apart, unless you drop it on your toe. However, when the children are grinding, they should be cautioned not to stick their fingers in the grinder.

Once they are introduced to taking the machines apart, most children want to do more. Remind them very strongly that they are not to take things apart at home or at school without an adult's permission.

EQUITY ISSUES

Try not to help the children put the grinders back together. Some groups will take longer than others to put the grinder into one piece, but almost all groups can do it, and the pride of "we did it all by ouselves" is very important. In addition, studies have shown that adults have a greater tendency to help girls perform manual tasks, e.g., using tools, woodworking. Therefore, it is especially important that girls be encouraged to problem-solve and meet the challenge of doing it themselves.

EXTENSIONS

Have the children make drawings of the pieces of the food grinder and label the order in which the pieces go back together.

If no food grinders are available, drip coffee pots, pencil sharpeners, or pepper mills can be used. If you have more than one grinder grating piece, use the different pieces and let the children see how different graters cause the food to come out in different shapes and sizes.

ACTIVITY IV

SETTING UP A TECHNOLOGY CENTER

PURPOSES

- To increase children's skills in working with tools.
- To increase all children's interest in tinkering.
- To encourage children to take machines apart to see how they work.

WHAT CHILDREN LEARN

- How to work with tools.
- What makes machines work.
- The fun of tinkering.

FORMAT

A. Large group discussion (10 minutes).
B. Individual and small group work (ongoing).

MATERIALS AND SUPPLIES

Spare machines with small numbers of large parts
e.g., food grinders, plant misters, hand drills with gears (and no bits), pepper mills, drip coffee pots, and anything with hinges

Small needle nose pliers

Phillips and slot screwdrivers of different sizes

Boxes of various sizes

Colored labels

Box for tools

BACKGROUND INFORMATION

It is important to know how the machines you select for the technology center work and how to take them apart and put them back together. For example:

> Plant misters — when one squeezes the bulb or handle of a plant mister, air is forced out of the tube. Water then rushes up to fill the empty tube (a partial vacuum) and out. A close look at the hole where the water comes out reveals that the edges are rough; this causes the stream of water to break up into a mist.

> Hand drills with gears — when you turn the handle, the teeth on the rest of the wheel turned by the handle hook into the teeth of a horizontal gear and turn it as well as the shaft with the drill bit in it. The turning and the pressure you apply cause a hole to be drilled. The size of the hole depends on the size of the bit used.

> Pepper mills — these work in much the same way as food grinders. As you turn the handle, the spiral core pushes the pepper against the graters or grinders. The pressure causes the pepper to push through the grinder holes and come out as small "chips" of pepper.

ACTIVITY

A. Large group discussion

1. Set up one machine in the technology center beforehand. The center should have its own tools and a tool box. Each machine should also have its own box. Each piece of a machine and its box should be coded with a label of the same color when there is more than one machine in the center, to keep the pieces together.

2. Gather the children around the technology center and talk about the machine that is there. Explain that this will be a part of the classroom and that everyone will be able to work in the center. Discuss how the tools should be used and this will help the children set up rules for the center. These may include:

- All parts must be put away in the correct box.
- Only one tool may be used at a time.
- Tools and machines must stay in the center.
- No running with tools in hand.

3. On successive days introduce additional machines and put them and their storage boxes in the technology center.

B. Individual and small group work (ongoing)

In the beginning, assign small groups of children to the technology center. Make sure that each child knows how to use the screwdrivers and pliers and at least tries the center. Later on use can be voluntary, as are the other centers, but keep an eye on it to be sure that both girls and boys use the center.

BE AWARE

After a stay in the technology center, few machines will work well. Therefore, don't use machines that have to be returned to owners. Check periodically for sharp and broken pieces and replace either the broken part or the machine. Remind the children very strongly that, outside of the technology center, they are not to take things apart at home or at school without an adult's permission.

Try to ensure that every child is comfortable working in the center. If you stay there and help children who need support and encouragement, those children will be more likely to try the center. Remember the teacher's presence in an area serves as a "magnet" to draw children to it.

EXTENSION

Change the machines in the technology center from time to time and have the children develop picture guides for putting the pieces back together. If parents agree, children can bring in items for the technology center that they are interested in investigating.

ACTIVITY V

TAKING
TECHNOLOGY
TRIPS

PURPOSES

• To provide a new perspective on class trips.

• To further increase children's awareness of the role machines play in our lives.

• To further increase all the children's interest in how machines work.

WHAT CHILDREN LEARN

• To recognize machines in the larger community.

• The different machines workers use.

• How some machines work.

FORMAT

A. Large group trip.

B. Large group discussion following trip (10 minutes).

MATERIALS AND SUPPLIES

Experience chart paper and markers

BACKGROUND INFORMATION

It is helpful to know about two or three machines that are used by the workers you will see on your field trip and to prepare some questions that can be asked about how the machines work. For example:

Sample Trips	Sample Machines	Sample Questions
Firehouse	Truck	How is the hose rolled and unrolled?
	Ladder	What makes the ladder go up?
	Pump	What makes the water go up?
Bank	Automatic Teller	How does it work?
	Coin counter	How does it tell the coins apart?
	Safe	How does the lock work?
Most trips	Typewriter	How does striking the keys make the letter print?
	Copying Machhine	What makes the paper go through?
School bus	Steering wheel	How does it make the wheels turn left and right?
	Ramp	How does it make it easier for people to get into the bus?
	Hydraulic lift for wheelchair accessibility	What makes it go up and down?

ACTIVITY

A. *Large group trip*

When setting up a trip, explain to the people at the site that a major focus of the trip is machines and how they work. Suggest a machine that children could see "in action." Request that the children be shown what the machine does and, as much as possible, how it works. You may want to provide the people at the site with some sample questions the children might ask such as those listed in *Background Information.*

Try to arrange a trip to a worksite where the worker who will demonstrate the machine is a person of color, female, and/or someone with a disability. This experience will serve to expand children's perceptions of who can and does work with machines.

Before the trip have a class discussion. Talk about what happens at a firehouse (or other site). Have the children talk about machines that they might see. If you are going to a firehouse, plan to look at the engine inside the hood of the truck.

B. *Large group discussion following trip*

1. When you return to the classroom, have a discussion about the machines you saw. Have the children use their imaginations to design other machines that the firehouse (or other site) might use. Make an experience chart to document the technology trip.

2. It may be that the questions the children asked will not have been answered during the trip. If that happens, with the children find out the answers by asking "experts," e.g., parents, school personnel, or by using reference books.

BE AWARE

Many times adults who provide information on a class trip, e.g., a postal worker or firefighter, are unfamiliar with preschoolers. Therefore, they may offer too much information in a style that is too technical for young children to absorb. Try to speak to the guide in advance, or if this is not feasible, be prepared to translate the information given into more age-appropriate language.

EQUITY ISSUES

If it is possible, request that a woman guide the tour and explain the technology. Experiences with actual role models do much to dispel stereotypes. Make the guide aware that you want all the children to understand technology and be comfortable with machines.

Guides are sometimes not aware of equity issues and give biased messages. If that happens, be prepared to respond. For example, if a guide says that only men should be firefighters because women don't have the strength, firmly explain that while some women will not have the strength neither will some men and thus strength, not sex, should be the basis for getting the job.

EXTENSIONS

Include a technology focus in all walks or trips. You might take the children to a supermarket where, in addition to food, children can learn about cash registers, scales, price scanners, automatic doors, and conveyor belts. You also might explore the school building in terms of technology.

The suggestion for technology trips comes from Dr. Selma Greenberg, School of Education, Hofstra University, Hempstead, N.Y.

RESOURCES

Math and Science at the Early Childhood Level

OVERVIEW

It is not easy to assemble math and science resources at the early childhood level. It is especially difficult to find age-appropriate materials that address the physical sciences and math concepts other than numbers. And, if one is looking for such materials that also are nonsexist, multicultural, and inclusive of people with disabilities, the task becomes even more difficult. Despite the recent thrust toward improving math and science education at all levels, many children's books about these topics date from the early 1960s when there was an earlier focus on math and science brought about by Sputnik. Although some of these books are fairly well balanced in their treatment of girls and boys, they are dated in the manner in which children and parents are depicted.

Wherever possible books for children have been selected that relate to the concepts that are addressed in this guide. Every attempt has been made to choose books that are nonsexist and represent a variety of cultures. Not one book on a math or science theme could be found that includes children with disabilities.

Other sections of this bibliography are Background Resources for Teachers and Parents, including books, booklets, and articles; and Additional Resources, including organizations that offer materials and information to help create an equitable math/science learning environment.

BOOKS FOR CHILDREN

Boston Section of the Society of Women Engineers. *Terry's Trip.* Boston: Boston Section—Society of Women Engineers (52 Poole Circle, Holbrook, MA 02343), 1982.

by the Boston Section of the Society of Women Engineers

Terry, an independent girl of about six, goes to visit her aunt and cousins in the city. She goes by herself on a train and is met by her Aunt Jennifer, who is an engineer. Terry visits the toy factory where Aunt Jennifer works and meets many different engineers who oversee production. Terry finds out that she will need to learn math, physics, and chemistry if she wants to become an engineer like her aunt. Simple black-and-white drawings and straightforward text make this a good introduction to science-related careers.

Bradbury, Lynne. Illustrated by Lynn N. Grundy. *Colors and Shapes.* Loughborough, England: Ladybird Books (U.S. distributor: Hutchinson Books, Lewiston, ME 04240), 1981.

A simple and colorful book about shapes; suitable for very young children. Very little text, but many intriguing illustrations of shapes, animals, and objects for children to identify.

Gibbons, Gail. *New Road!* New York: Thomas Y. Crowell, 1983.

Explains the technology used in building a road and shows many tools and machines in operation. Females and males read plans, use surveying tools and computers, and drive heavy machinery. Bright, four-color illustrations are multicultural as well as nonsexist. *New Road!* is part of a series by Gail Gibbons that includes *The Post Office Book.*

Homan, Dianne. Illustrated by Mary Heine. *In Christina's Toolbox.* Chapel Hill: Lollipop Power, Inc. (P.O. Box 1171, Chapel Hill, NC 27514), 1981.

Christina uses the tools in her toolbox to construct a bird feeder. She is shown sawing, measuring, hammering, and using a screwdriver. Christina is active and capable and enjoys using tools just as her mother does. The book portrays a Black family in nonstereotypical sex roles.

Hoban, Tana. *Circles, Triangles and Squares.* New York: Macmillan Publishing Company, 1974.

This prize-winning book contains no text but features a fine series of black-and-white photos by Tana Hoban depicting circles, triangles, and squares in the environment. The cover features two girls drawing figures using shapes, and multicultural pictures of active girls appear throughout.

Lenthall, Patricia Riley. Illustrated by the author. *Carlotta and the Scientist.* Chapel Hill: Lollipop Power, Inc., 1973.

Carlotta is a penquin who sets out to gather food for her family. On her way, she finds an injured scientist and helps her back to her base camp. While Carlotta is away, her mate nurtures their egg until their baby penguin hatches. Offers nonstereotypical views of male and female roles and interesting information on Emperor penguins.

Lionni, Leo. Illustrated by the author. *Inch by Inch.* New York: Astor-Honor, Inc., 1960.

An inch worm about to be eaten by a robin proves its worth by measuring the robin's tail and various parts of other birds. A fun introduction to measurement that could be followed by activities with rules, strings, blocks, and other forms of measurement. Unfortunately, both the robin and the inch worm are referred to as "he." Beautiful, soft-colored drawings by Lionni.

Lionni, Leo. Illustrated by the author. *Little Blue and Little Yellow.* New York: Astor Books, 1959.

A classic about what happens when colors mix: circles of blue and yellow become green, and they are not recognized by their respective parents when they come home. Again, even the two circles that are the main characters of this book are referred to as "he"! Otherwise, the book is a fine introduction to the chemistry of color mixing.

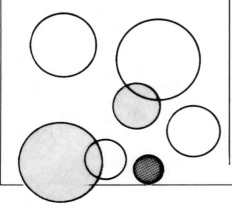

Mandell, Muriel. Illustrated by S. Matsuda. *Physics Experiments for Children.* New York: Dover Publications, Inc., 1959.

Contains experiments to do with machines, heat, sound, light, and magnetism and electricity. Although the book is meant to be used independently by elementary school age children, early childhood teachers can easily adapt some of the activities for use with preschool children.

Podendorf, Illa. Illustrated by Frances Eckart. *Change and Time.* Chicago: Childrens Press, 1971.

A book about physical changes in solids, liquids, and gases that go on around us all the time. Changes caused by temperature, evaporation, friction, and light are discussed. Although the illustrations are dated, they are multiracial, and girls and boys are fairly well balanced.

Schneider, Herman, and Schneider, Nina. Illustrations by Harriet Sherman. *Science Fun with a Flashlight.* New York: McGraw-Hill Book Company, 1975.

A group of children at a costume party experiment with flashlights after a power failure. The book then goes on to describe a variety of nighttime and daytime shadow activities. Illustrations are multiracial, and there is a fairly good balance of girls and boys.

Srivastava, Jane Jonas. Illustrated by Aliki. *Weighing and Balancing* (Young Math Books). New York: Thomas Y. Crowell Company, 1970.

An introduction to weighing and balancing. Describes some of the history of weighing things by hand and the development of scales and fixed measurements such as the pound. The illustrations are multiracial, and some active girls are depicted. Males, however, predominate. This book is part of a series developed at the University of Illinois. Other titles include *Estimation, And What is Symmetry?,* and *How Did Numbers Begin?*

Wahl, John, and Whal, Stacy. *I Can Count the Petals of a Flower.* Reston, VA: National Council of Teachers of Mathematics, Inc.

(1906 Association Dr., Reston VA 22091), 1976.

Beautiful color photographs of flowers having from one to ten petals. Combinations of flowers are used to count up to sixteen petals. Children learn to keep track as they count the petals in a circle. Four large posters taken from the book's illustrations also are available.

Zaslavsky, Claudia. Illustrated by Jerry Pinkney. *Count on Your Fingers African Style.* New York: Thomas Y. Crowell, 1980.

Finger counting is a practical strategy in the African marketplace, where people who speak many different languages come together to trade. This simple book, illustrated with highly authentic black-and-white drawings of African people from many countries, helps children understand the practical uses of mathematics.

BACKGROUND RESOURCES FOR TEACHERS AND PARENTS

BOOKS/BOOKLETS

Brenner, Barbara, and Endreweit, Maries. *Bank Street Family Computer Book.* New York: Ballantine Books, 1984.

An easy-to-use introduction to computers for the whole family. Practical information is offered in nontechnical language. Contains a useful bibliography of selected software for children age three and up. Unfortunately, the cartoon illustrations are extremely sex-stereotyped.

Brown, Sam Ed. Illustrations by Silas Stamper. *Bubbles Rainbows and Worms: Science Experi-* *ments for Pre-School Children.* Mt. Rainier, MD: Gryphon House (P.O. Box 275, Mt. Rainier, MD 20712), 1981.

A very easy-to-use format and a broad range of science activities. Stresses the importance of early childhood science. Two drawbacks — in the illustrations that feature children, boys predominate and have the more active roles. (The one picture that features two girls shows them dressing up to illustrate an activity about the seasons.) Also, the illustrations are of white children only.

Brown, Sam Ed. Illustrations by Jula Libonn. *One, Two, Buckle My Shoe: Math Activities for Young Children.* Mt. Rainier, MD: Gryphon House, Inc., 1982.

Very simple and familiar math activities for one-to-one correspondence, counting, matching, measuring shapes, sequencing, and other beginning mathematical concepts. The illustrations are multicultural, but the generic "he" is used even when an illustration features a girl.

Downie, Diane, Slesnick, Twila and Stenmark, Jean Kerr. *Math for Girls and Other Problem Solvers.* Berkeley: Lawrence Hall of Science, University of California, 1981.

Activities especially designed to develop visual-spatial and problem-solving skills in girls so they will not avoid math courses later on. Since the activities are geared for children 6-14 years of age, not all the activities are age-appropriate, and even the simplest one will have to be scaled down for preschool children. The photographs are multiracial, but the drawn illustrations are all of children who are white.

Holt, Bess-Gene et al. *Getting Involved: Your Child and Science.* Washington, DC: Office of Human Development Services, Administration for Children, Youth and Families, Head Start Bureau. Issued Nov. 1981, reprinted 1983. DHHS Publication Number (OHDS) 83-31143.

A booklet explaining simple ways that parents can introduce children to science through experiences found in the home and nearby community. Presents a balanced view of girls and boys participating in science-related activities. Other booklets in the series include *Your Child and Math, Your Child and Problem-Solving,* and *Your Child's Attitude Toward Learning.* Unfortunately, while the information is good, these latter booklets cannot be recommended because, unlike the science booklet, the illustrations are sexist, featuring many more males than females involved in activitites.

Jameson, Valerie. *Scholastic Early Childhood Program: Mathematics Teaching Guide.* New York: Scholastic Book Services, 1981.

A comprehensive guide to a full year of excellent and varied math activities for preschool and kindergarten. Activities are centered around themes such as Same and Different, Needs and Feelings, Work and Play, and Growth and Change. The teaching guide is nonsexist, multicultural, and includes children with disabilities. Although it is part of a larger program that included hands-on materials and assessment

instruments, the guide is available separately from Scholastic, Inc., P.O. Box 7501, 2931 East McCarty, Jefferson City, MO 65102. The guide is expensive, but schools get a 25 percent discount, and it would be an excellent addition to a teacher resources collection.

Kamii, Constance. *Number in Preschool and Kindergarten: Educational Implications of Piaget's Theory.* Washington, DC: National Association for the Education of Young Children, 1982.

A practical interpretation of Piaget's theories about how children learn to understand numerical concepts as applied to preschool. Makes a strong case for encouraging a child to think actively and autonomously, learning to construct numbers rather than to produce "right" answers. The generic "he" is used throughout, which is unfortunate since the active, problem-solving approach is essential for all children.

Mitchell, Lucy Sprague, *Young Geographers.* New York: Bank Street College of Education, 1971.

First published in 1934, this small book is a classic about how to help young children understand spatial relationships through exploring the environment in which they live.

Map-making and charting ideas, trips, and block-building schemes are described and discussed.

Myers, Helen. *Scholastic Early Childhood Program: Science Teaching Guide.* New York: Scholastic Book Services, 1981.

A companion to the *Mathematics Teaching Guide* described above. Activities are centered around the same themes of Same and Different, Needs and Feelings, Work and Play, and Growth and Change. Basic science concepts are covered in age-appropriate, interesting activities that range from simple to more complex. Illustrations are nonsexist, multicultural, and include children with disabilities. Includes an extensive resource guide. For ordering information see Jameson, Valerie, *Scholastic Early Childhood Program: Mathematics Teaching Guide.*

Nuffield Mathematics Project. *Environmental Geometry.* New York: John Wiley and Sons, Inc., 1969.

Interesting and practical ideas for helping children become aware of shapes in the environment and the relationship of form to function. Girls and boys are shown manipulating materials, building outdoor structures, and constructing models of variously shaped buildings. *Mathematics Begins,* Level 1 (1967) is another part of the Nuffield Mathematics Project that offers interesting and age-appropriate math activities. Contains good ideas for making sets, graphs, and one-to-one correspondence charts.

Zaslavsky, Claudia. *Preparing Young Children for Math.* New York: Schocken Books, 1979.

Simple ideas for games and activities parents and teachers can use to introduce math concepts to young children. The importance of allowing children to make mistakes and of taking time to understand the thinking process that has led to the mistake is discussed. Games are arranged in three areas: Shape and Space, Comparing and Measuring, and Numbers. In referring to children, "he" and "she" are used alternately.

Zubrowski, Bernie. Illustrated by Joan Dressler. *Bubbles.* Boston: Little Brown and Company, 1979.

This Children's Museum Activity Book is part of a science series issued by the Boston Children's Museum. Although the book is written for elementary school students, it is full of ideas for exploring bubbles that can be adapted for the early childhood level. Other books by Bernie Zubrowski include: *Messing Around with Baking Chemistry,* illustrated by Signe Hanson, and *Messing Around with Water Pumps and Siphone,* illustrated by Steve Lindblom.

ARTICLES

Barnes, B.J., and Hill, Shirley. "Should Young Children Work with Microcomputers — Logo Before Lego?" *The Computing Teacher,* May 1983, pp. 11-14.

Raises some important questions about young children's ability to use computers to maximum advantage given their preoperational learning styles. Stresses the importance of experiential learning.

Burg, Karen. "The Microcomputer in the Kindergarten." *Young Children* (The Journal of the National Association for the Education of Young Children), vol. 39, no. 3, March 1984, pp. 28-33.

A cautious yet positive view of selective use of the computer in the kindergarten. Burg advocates individualized programs designed for the needs of particular children. She is careful to incorporate computer activities into a daily program that stresses the value of experiential learning.

Campbell, Patricia B. "Computers and Children: Eliminating Discrimination Before It Takes Hold." *Equal Play,* vol. IV, nos. 1 & 2, Spring/Fall 1983, pp.4-7 (Women's Action Alliance, 370 Lexington Ave., New York 10017).

As computers become more prevalent in schools, inequities in their use are arising. Girls program less frequently than boys, boys dominate the use of the computers, and software programs are geared toward boys' interests. The article discusses the issues and offers strategies for creating computer equity in the classroom.

Cuffaro, Harriet K. "Microcomputers in Education: Why Is Earlier Better?" *Teachers' College Record,* vol. 85, no. 4, Summer 1984, pp 559-568.

This article questions the appropriateness of computers and available software in the early childhood classroom. Citing what is known about young children's preoperational learning styles as defined by Piaget and the value of experiential learning as defined by John Dewey, Cuffaro argues that at about age eight, when children enter the concrete operational level, they are

better able to take full advantage of the challenges that computers and programming may offer.

Greenberg, Selma. "Educational Equity in Early Childhood Environments." In *Handbook for Achieving Sex Equity Through Education,* edited by Sue Klein. Baltimore: The Johns Hopkins University Press, 1985, pp. 457-469.

A discussion of the sex-differentiated learning attributes with which children enter preschool and the resulting deficit areas of learning that result. Contains valuable parent/teacher strategies for making early learning more equitable. (Also see Introduction to this guide.)

Jacobs, Janie E., and Eccles, Jaquelynne S. "Gender Differences in Math Mobility: The Impact of Media Reports on Parents." *Educational Researcher,* vol. 14, no. 3, March 1985, pp. 20-24.

A study of how media coverage of educational research influences perceptions. Parents were surveyed regarding their children's math abilities before and after being exposed to media coverage. Mothers of daughters and fathers of sons became more stereotyped in their beliefs. But, unexpectedly, media exposure had a positive effect on fathers of daughters; these fathers came to the defense of their daughters.

Serbin, Lisa. "Play Activities and the Development of Visual-Spatial Skills." *Equal Play,* vol. I, no. 4, Fall 1980, pp. 6-8 (Women's Action Alliance, 370 Lexington Ave., New York, NY 10017).

This article underscores the importance of providing practice in visual-spatial activities for those children (usually girls) who don't self-select activities in this area of the curriculum. (Also see Introduction to this guide.)

"Students Know More Science But Boys Still Do Better," *The Newsletter of Teachers College/Columbia University,* vol. 13, no. 2, Spring 1985, pp. 4-5.

Findings of the Second International Science Study (1983) reveal that while students have stronger science backgrounds now than they did 15 years ago, boys outperform girls at every level, especially in the physical sciences. Citing the gender gap, the study suggests that girls might benefit from more handling of physical materials, e.g., balls, flashlights, and aquariums. More female role models and home-based science experiences also are suggested as ways to help girls become more comfortable with the physical sciences.

ADDITIONAL RESOURCES

Center for Children and Technology, Bank Street College of Education, 610 West 112th St., New York, NY 10025.

A major resource for research on the uses and effects of computers in the elementary classroom. The Center has many reports available on research conducted since the mid-1970s. Based on research, Bank Street has recommended that computers be introduced beginning at the third grade level.

Ciba-Geigy Corporation, Ardsley, NY 10502.

Publishes a poster and accompanying booklet, "Exceptional Black Scientists," featuring the work of women and men. Available free from the Corporate Relations Department.

General Electric Company, Fairfield, CT 06431.

GE offers a series of booklets about various career options in science and technology. Four-color pictures feature women and men in a variety of jobs ranging from skilled technician to management. These nonsexist, multicultural booklets provide wonderful pictures for collages, bulletin boards, and other activities about what scientists do. Available free from the Educational Communications Program.

Math/Science Network, Lawrence Hall of Science, University of California, Berkeley, CA 94720.

The Math/Science Network is an association of 800 scientists, educators, engineers, community leaders, and parents who work cooperatively to increase the number of women interested in and qualified for scientific and technical careers. The Network provides support and coordination for programs designed for students of all ages, educators and parents, women resuming scientific work, and professional scientists and engineers. For more information write to Nancy Kreinberg, Director. (Also see Downie et al, Teacher/Parent Resources.)

National Council of Teachers of Mathematics, 1906 Association Drive, Reston, VA 22091.

This major professional organization for mathematics teachers publishes the *Journal for Research in Mathematics Education,* holds an annual national conference, and publishes resources. Although the membership concentrates on the elementary and secondary levels, they do have some early childhood resources such as *I Can Count the Petals of a Flower* (see Wahl and Wahl, Children's Math and Science Books).

National Science Foundation, 1800 G St. N.W., Washington, DC 20550.

Offers booklets, statistics, and other resources on women and people of color in the fields of science and engineering.

National Science Teachers Association, 1742 Connecticut Ave. N.W., Washington, DC 20009.

This professional membership organization publishes a fine magazine called *Science and Children.* Although it is primarily geared to elementary science, there is a regular early childhood column, and many pictures and ideas can be adapted for use in the early childhood classroom. The organization also has a *Women Scientists Roster* listing 1,300 career role models by state and speciality.

Research Triangle Institute, P.O. Box 12194, Research Triangle Park, NC 27709.

This group offers a series of 15 large posters featuring photos and biographies of scientists. The set is outstanding since it is nonsexist, multicultural, and includes scientists with disabilities.

TABS, Aids for Ending Sexism in School, 744 Carroll St., Brooklyn, NY 11215.

TABS sells a series of posters featuring women. Those most relevant for creating a science environment include Madame Curie and Science Jobs, which features a girl thinking about all the jobs that scientists do. Catalog available.

Women's Educational Equity Act Publishing center, Educational Development Corporation, Inc., 55 Chapel St. Newton, MA 02160.

Although most of the math and science programs funded by the Women's Educational Equity Act Program have focused on secondary students, some of the materials might be adaptable or provide resources for early childhood programs.

ORGANIZATIONS

The following organizations are sources for information about women, people of color, and people with disabilities in the fields of math, science, and technology:

American Association for the Advancement of Science, 1515 Massachusetts Ave., N.W., Washington, DC 20005. Distributes a *"Resource Directory of Handicapped Scientists"* and many career materials.

American Chemical Society, 1155 16th St., N.W., Washington, DC 20036. Write to Allen McClelland, Education Committee.

American Physical Society, 335 West 45th St., New York, NY 10017. The Committee on the Status of Women in Physics.

The Association for Women in Science, P.O. Box 13, Lemont, IL 60439.

Society of Women Engineers, 345 East 47th St., New York, NY 10017

Women and Mathematics, c/o Carole B. Lacampagne, Department of Mathematics, University of Michigan, Flint, MI 48153.

ABOUT THE AUTHORS

Barbara Sprung is co-director of Educational Equity Concepts, Inc., a national nonprofit organization she co-founded with Merle Froschl in 1982. She served as project director of Beginning Math and Science Equitably in 1983-1984 and currently directs Be a Scientist!, a program to develop science activity kits for grades 4-6 based on the work of women scientists.

In 1972 Ms. Sprung was the founding director of the Non-Sexist Child Development Project at the Women's Action Alliance, Inc. Since that time, she has been a pioneer in the development of early childhood programs and materials that are nonsexist, multicultural, and inclusive of images of children and adults with disabilities. She was the developer of My Family and Community Helpers block accessory figures, Play Scenes Lotto, First Readings About My Family and My School, Community Careers Flannel Board, People at Work and Men in Nurturing Roles photo sets, Resources Photos for Mainstreaming, and puzzles of Men in Nurturing Roles. She is a much sought-after speaker and has written extensively for journals and popular magazines. Ms. Sprung is the author of *Non-Sexist Education for Young Children: A Practical Guide* and *Creating a New Mainstream: An Early Childhood Training Manual for an "Inclusionary" Curriculum,* co-author of *Including All of Us: An Early Childhood Curriculum About Disability,* and editor of *Perspectives on Non-Sexist Early Childhood Education.* Ms. Sprung received a Bachelor of Arts in Early Childhood Education from Sarah Lawrence College and a Masters in Child Development from Bank Street College of Education.

Merle Froschl, co-director of Educational Equity Concepts, Inc., was director of the Non-Sexist Child Development Project from 1980-1982 where she directed Project R.E.E.D. (Resources on Educational Equity for the Disabled) and Beginning Equal: The Project on Non-Sexist Childrearing for Infants and Toddlers. From

1973-1979, Merle Froschl was director of educational services at The Feminist Press, editor of the second edition of *Feminist Resources for Schools and Colleges: A Guide to Curricular Materials,* and field testing director of the "Women's Lives/Women's Work" series.

Ms. Froschl has a Bachelor of Arts degree in Journalism from Syracuse University and has written extensively on issues of educational equity for professional journals and the popular press. She has conducted inservice training, given workshop presentations, and lectured widely at conferences and professional meetings for more than a dozen years. Most recently, she was director of Project Inclusive and co-author of *Including All of Us: An Early Childhood Curriculum About Disability;* co-coordinator of the Women and Disability Awareness Project, and one of the authors of *Building Community: A Manual Exploring Issues of Women and Disability.* Ms. Froschl participated in the development and implementation of Beginning Math and Science Equitably and currently is materials developer for Be a Scientist!, a project to develop science activity kits for grades 4-6 based on the work of women scientists.

Patricia B. Campbell directs Campbell-Kibler Associates, a consulting firm specializing in materials development, educational evaluation, and equity projects. She has been a consultant to Educational Equity Concepts, Inc. since its inception. In addition to designing the evaluation components of several projects, Dr. Campbell has been part of the development team of Project Inclusive, Beginning Math and Science Equitably, and Be a Scientist! Dr. Campbell holds a B.S. in Mathematics from LeMoyne College, an M.S. in Instructional Technology from Syracuse University, and a Ph.D. in Teacher Education, also from Syracuse. She was Assistant Associate Professor of Research, Measurement and Statistics at Georgia State University from 1973-1977.

In addition to her work with Educational Equity Concepts, Inc., Dr. Campbell is developing The Right Start, an elementary science and technology curriculum with Dr. Selma Greenberg of Hofstra University; "A Headstart for Head Start", a multimedia pilot project to introduce Head Start children to computers; "The Computer World: Open to You" a media and software package to involve upper elementary girls and boys with computers; and "The Hidden Discrimination: Bias in Research Methods," a project to increase educators' awareness of how racism, sexism, and other societal biases influence educational research. Dr. Campbell has published more than sixty articles, monographs, and book chapters on a variety of educational equity topics.

ABOUT EDUCATIONAL EQUITY CONCEPTS, INC.

Educational Equity Concepts, Inc. is a national, nonprofit organization founded in 1982 to foster the development of children and adults through advancing educational excellence and equity. The organization creates educational programs and materials that are free of sex, race, and disability bias; offers training programs for parents, teachers, and students; and engages in a variety of public education activities.

One of our basic philosophical tenets is to "begin at the beginning." To this end, we are engaged in a variety of early childhood projects. Currently, our early childhood programs emphasize math, science, and mainstreaming, and we are developing classroom resources such as block accessories and curriculum guides.

Educational Equity Concepts also is concerned with maximizing the opportunities of adults who have not had the chance to "begin early." In this area, we focus on programs to help women with disabilities and women of color achieve educational equity and develop their full potential.

In all of our programs, Educational Equity Concepts' approach is "inclusive," making the connection between various factors that can limit individual growth and protential. *What Will Happen If . . . Young Children and the Scientific Method* is a direct result of that endeavor. By ensuring that *all* children have equal opportunities to learn essential math and science skills we help them to develop their potential unlimited by bias due to sex, race, or disability.